WHEN
THE
KILLER
MAN
COMES

WHEN THE KILLER MAN COMES

ELIMINATING TERRORISTS
AS A SPECIAL OPERATIONS SNIPER

PAUL MARTINEZ

WITH

GEORGE GALDORISI

ST. MARTIN'S PRESS ≋ NEW YORK

www.stmartins.com

Designed by Omar Chapa

The Library of Congress Cataloging-in-Publication Data is available upon request.

ISBN 978-1-250-09440-7 (hardcover)
ISBN 978-1-250-09441-4 (ebook)

Our books may be purchased in bulk for promotional, educational, or business use. Please contact your local bookseller or the Macmillan Corporate and Premium Sales Department at 1-800-221-7945, extension 5442, or by email at MacmillanSpecialMarkets@macmillan.com.

First Edition: October 2018

10 9 8 7 6 5 4 3 2 1

This book is dedicated to the men and women I served with. You are a mighty and compassionate force, pitted against an evil so terrible that past generations must be conscripted to face it.

You are the greatest generation, and to walk among you was to walk among giants. Thank you for counting me among your honored numbers.

And to my family, both of blood and of the covenant, without whom I most certainly would have given in to my lesser nature, never returning from the abyss I so loved to gaze upon.

May our fallen never be forgotten, may our deeds be told for ages, and may those of us still living never succumb to our wounds.

Below, listed in reverse chronological order, are those Rangers of 75th Ranger Regiment killed during the War on Terror, as well as the SEALS I had the honor of serving with who also perished in this conflict, along with their aircrew of CH-47D Extortion 17, who perished on August 6, 2011, while attempting to relieve their brothers who were in desperate conflict with the enemy.

The friends that we have lost do not repose in the bosom of the earth, but are buried deep in our hearts, and it has been thus ordained that we may always be accompanied by them.

—Alexandre Dumas,
The Count of Monte Cristo

BATTALIONS

1ST BN

SGT Justin B. Allen

SPC Marc A. Anderson

CPL Matthew A. Commons

SGT Bradley S. Crose

SSG Jason S. Dahlke

SPC Joseph W. Dimock II

PFC Eric W. Hario

SGT Tanner S. Higgins

SSG Jeremy A. Katzenberger

SGT Martin A. Logo

SSG Kevin Pape

SGT Jonathan K. Peney

SGT Alessandro L. Plutino

SGT Roberto D. Sanchez

SFC Lance H. Vogeler

SPC Christopher S. Wright

SSG Anthony D. Davis

2ND BN

SGT Jay A. Blessing

SPC Ricardo Cerros Jr

SGT Joel D. Clarkson

SFC Kristoffer B. Domeij

SPC Christopher Gathercole

SGT Tyler Nicholas Holtz

PFC Christopher A. Horns

SPC George V. Libby

SGT Thomas R. MacPherson

SFC David L. McDowell

CPL Patrick D. Tillman

SSG Ricardo Barraza

SGT Dale G. Brehm

SPC Thomas F. Duncan III

CPL Jason Kessler

PFC Nathan E. Stahl

3RD BN

CPL William M. Amundsen

CPT Kyle A. Comfort

SPC Ryan C. Garbs

PFC Damian J. Garza

SGT Patrick C. Hawkins

PVT John M. Henderson

CPL Michael D. Jankiewicz

CPL Benjamin S. Kopp

SGT Ronald Kubrick

SGT Andrew C. Nicol

SGT Michael C. O'Neil

PFC Cody J. Patterson

SPC Bradley D. Rappuhn

SGT Anibal Santiago

SGT Jason A. Santora

PFC Kristofer D. S. Thomas

MSG Jared N. Van Aalst

CPL Andrew F. Chris

SGT Timothy M. Conneway

CPL Benjamin C. Dillon

SGT Steven C. Ganczeski

PFC Dillon Jutras

SSG Nino Livaudais

SPC Ryan Long

CPL Ryan McGhee

SSG James R. Patton

SGT James J. Regan

CPT Russel B. Rippetoe

SGT William P. Rudd

CPL Timothy M. Shea

SGT Cameron H. Thomas

SGT Joshua P. Rodgers

PFC Kristofor T. Stonesifer

SPC John Joseph Edmunds

EXTORTION 17

SGT Alexander J. Bennett

SPC Spencer Duncan

CWO Bryan J. Nichols

CWO David R. Carter

SSG Patrick D. Hamburger

TSgt John W. Brown

SSgt Andrew W. Harvell

TSgt Daniel L. Zerbe

PO1(SEAL) Darrick C. Benson

CPO(SEAL) Brian R. Bill

PO1(SEAL) Christopher G. Campbell

PO1 Jared W. Day

PO1 John Douangdara and Navy SEAL Dog "Bart"

CPO(SEAL) John W. Faas

CPO(SEAL) Kevin A. Houston

Lt. Cmdr.(SEAL) Jonas B. Kelsall

MCPO(SEAL) Louis J. Langlais

CPO(SEAL) Matthew D. Mason

CPO(SEAL) Stephen M. Mills

CPO Nicholas H. Null

PO1(SEAL) Jesse D. Pittman

SCPO(SEAL) Thomas A. Ratzlaff

CPO(SEAL) Robert J. Reeves

CPO(SEAL) Heath M. Robinson

PO2(SEAL) Nicholas P. Spehar

PO1 Michael J. Strange

PO1(SEAL) Jon T. Tumilson

PO1(SEAL) Aaron C. Vaughn

SCPO Kraig M. Vickers

PO1(SEAL) Jason R. Workman

Find what you love, and let it kill you.

—*Charles Bukowski*

CONTENTS

Editor's Note on Names xvii

Foreword xix

Preface xxv

1. Chechen Sniper 1
2. Night Ops 40
3. Sugar Shack 72
4. Working with the DEA 91
5. Saving the Cavalry 131
6. Castle Mission 166
7. Simo Shot 195
8. Tangi Valley 223
9. Eye on the Prize 247

Acknowledgments 263

EDITOR'S NOTE ON NAMES

In spite of the brave exploits of men like Paul Martinez and those he served with, the United States is still engaged in the Global War on Terrorism in places like Iraq and Afghanistan. This means that many of the men whose deeds are described in this book are still serving overseas.

These warriors would be in additional jeopardy if their names were revealed in these pages. For this reason, Paul has used pseudonyms to protect their anonymity, as well as to ensure their continued operational viability.

FOREWORD

America has one force with the single mission of direct action to capture or kill the enemy: the 75th Ranger Regiment. This special operations force—part of the U.S. Army Special Operations Command—is a unique and distinct entity within the U.S. military. No other unit in any other U.S. military service has this singular mission of direct action.

Rangers stand alone as the most active brigade-size unit in the U.S. Special Operations Command, the lead U.S. combatant command engaged in the Global War on Terrorism. Since 9/11, the 75th Ranger Regiment has been the only continuously engaged unit in the U.S. Army, and for the last decade and a half, 40 percent of those deployed have been in harm's way. Their mission is unique. Rangers don't patrol, don't train allied forces, and don't engage in routine counterinsurgency duties. They have a single focus: to seek out the enemy and capture or kill them.

Today's 75th Ranger Regiment traces its roots to the century before the American Revolution, when colonists in Maryland and Virginia began to organize groups of men to patrol the perimeters of their holdings as a means of early warning of Indian attacks. In 1675—a full century before America's war for independence—in response to attacks by the Wampanoag, the governor of the Plymouth Colony had Benjamin Church raise a company of men to conduct scouting and raiding actions against the tribe. Church's written reports included the phrase "Today we ranged out four miles to the west," and thus the word "Ranger" was born.

The term Ranger was used again during the French and Indian Wars, which pitted the New England colonists against the French Canadians. The first Ranger Company was formed by a frontiersman named Robert Rogers. Rogers went on to form nine additional units. These ten companies took the fight for the British cause deep into French territory. Robert Rogers's *Ranger Standing Orders*, written in 1759, is quoted in the *Ranger's Handbook*, which is issued to every U.S. Army Ranger today.

The Rangers continued to lead the way in America's wars. In 1775, the Continental Congress authorized the formation of a number of companies of expert riflemen. General George Washington called these companies his "Corps of Rangers." During the Revolutionary War, Colonel Francis Marion, widely known as the "Swamp Fox," conducted direct-action raids against the British Army, a harbinger of today's Ranger operations.

Ranger campaigns continued in the following century. In 1835, the General Counsel of the provisional government formed the "Corps of Rangers" to protect settlers of the fledgling republic from marauding Comanche. This force then played a prominent role during the struggle for Texas independence, and later in the Mexican-American War.

In the Civil War, both the Union and the Confederacy used Rangers to take the fight behind enemy lines. The exploits of the Confederate Ranger John Mosby, known as the "Gray Ghost," provided another link in the chain to today's Rangers. Following the Civil War and through the First World War, Rangers as we know them today all but disappeared from the American military. They resurfaced prominently in World War II.

When the United States entered the War after the December 7, 1941, attack on Pearl Harbor, the country had a peacetime army and no special operations units. Army Chief of Staff General George Marshall authorized the establishment of the 1st Ranger Battalion the following year. Six additional Ranger Battalions were formed during the War, where they served with distinction first in the North African and European campaigns and later in the conflict in the Pacific.

The exploits of the Rangers in World War II have been well chronicled in books and film, and their courageous actions have become part of the military—and, indeed, national—lexicon. From the Boys of Pointe du Hoc during the Normandy invasion to Darby's Rangers in Italy to Merrill's Marauders in the Pacific, Rangers have taken the fight to the enemy. U.S. Army Rangers continued to distinguish themselves in direct action in the conflicts in Korea and Vietnam.

Darby's Rangers deserve special mention. Colonel William Orlando Darby was killed while leading what came to be known as Task Force Darby, part of the Army's 10th Mountain Division, spearheading the breakout of the U.S. Fifth Army from the Po River Valley bridgehead, where they were pitted against a large German force. Task Force Darby was sent on a crucial mission against overwhelming odds and walked into an ambush. That tradition will play out in these pages as Paul Martinez tells his story.

Today's 75th Ranger Regiment was formally established in 1984 at Fort Benning, Georgia. Since that time, Rangers have fought in every American conflict: Desert Storm (Iraq, 1991), Restore Hope (Somalia, 1993), Uphold Democracy (Haiti, 1994), and Joint Guardian (Kosovo, 1999). They currently fight in the Global War on Terrorism.

I talked about the 75th Ranger Regiment's actions to ensure America's security and prosperity in my books *The Reaper* (St. Martin's Press, 2015) and *Way of the Reaper* (St. Martin's Press, 2016). Working as an Army Ranger sniper in Iraq and Afghanistan was my way of serving my country, fighting terrorists who would do our nation harm.

I finished my service as a Ranger sniper in the 75th Ranger Regiment and moved on to other pursuits partly because I felt the war in Afghanistan was winding down. That would mean the need for the U.S. military, the Rangers, and especially Ranger snipers would diminish, to the point where I thought I would never face the intense operations I had experienced during my years in uniform. I was wrong. It turned out I missed the most intense action in the Global War on Terrorism.

Soon after I completed my time as a Ranger sniper, our nation made the decision to withdraw from Afghanistan in two years. The intention was good, but there were still a large number of senior Taliban and al-Qaeda leaders and other terrorists in secure locations throughout the country, especially in areas near the border with Pakistan. If the United States was to withdraw from Afghanistan with these terrorists and their networks still intact, they could quickly take over the country and undo all the gains we had made there.

These guys needed to be eliminated, and there was only one force to do it: the Rangers. The mission to capture or kill these terrorists was assigned to the 3rd Ranger Battalion of the 75th Ranger Regiment. Naming this unit "Team Merrill," after the Marauders of World War II fame, was prophetic. These Rangers faced near-impossible odds taking on an enemy who knew they were coming and employed every conceivable tactic to kill them.

Team Merrill fought for seven months deep in enemy territory, and like their World War II predecessors, these twenty-first-century Rangers accomplished their mission and beat down the terrorist threat. In doing so, Team Merrill became the lynchpin of the U.S. counterterror/counterinsurgency strategy in Afghanistan.

My friend Paul Martinez was part of that team, and what he did as a Ranger sniper in Afghanistan helped turn the tide of that conflict in our favor. His experience in these high-risk/high-reward missions—in many cases, efforts that faced near-impossible odds—is a story we've all been waiting to hear. I'll stop here and let Paul tell you this story in his own words.

—*Nicholas Irving*
San Antonio, Texas

PREFACE

He who makes a beast of himself gets rid of the
pain of being a man.

—*Samuel Johnson*

I grew up in Colorado and, like many young guys, dreamed
of adventure. My earliest memories are of wanting to be
an astronaut, a fighter pilot, or a sniper. And I was raised
with a deep respect for the U.S. military, believing that
everyone from Audie Murphy to the doctors in *M*A*S*H*
to the men who received the Medal of Honor for their he-
roics in Iraq and Afghanistan was a hero and a good
American.

Right out of high school, I didn't feel the calling to
join the U.S. military. It's probably because I didn't see the
point of being in the peacetime Army. Sure, the United
States was fighting in Iraq and Afghanistan, but everyone
was saying that all would be over soon. Little did we know
how long those conflicts would last. Instead, I worked in

the tech industry and in construction, not knowing exactly what I wanted to do with my life.

Then things changed. I had several close friends come back from Operation Iraqi Freedom with ghosts in their eyes and gravel in their voices. They didn't make it sound like we'd be out of Iraq or Afghanistan anytime soon. Suddenly, the war sounded very real, and my reluctance to be part of a peacetime Army faded away. Now I knew we weren't at peace, and I felt that if we didn't stand together as friends, as brothers, and as a country, we might not make it.

I walked into a recruiter's office in Westminster, Colorado, in December 2005 knowing only that I wanted to join the Army and get to the fight. When I learned I could qualify for an Airborne contract I was sold, and in April 2006 I was in the Army and shipped out for Army infantry basic training at Fort Benning, Georgia. Next came individual training for my military occupational specialty (MOS) as an indirect fire infantryman. What that meant was that I was a mortar man. (One of the decisions I made when I decided to write this book was not to dazzle you with military acronyms, but to use them as I would in normal conversation and then explain what they stand for.)

From there it was on to Army Airborne School—otherwise known as "Jump School"—also at Fort Benning. Things were settling in as I was finishing Jump School, and got my orders to my first unit, the 173rd Airborne Brigade Combat Team—the "Sky Soldiers"—in beautiful Vicenza, Italy.

I was still training at Fort Benning and looking forward to my overseas assignment when my best buddy from basic training, "Easy" Esenzimmer, dropped by my barracks and said he had to go to a Ranger Indoctrination Program briefing. In the Army, you don't go anywhere without a buddy, so I tagged along. I have to admit, though, that it was more than just keeping a buddy company.

I think I always knew I wanted to be a Ranger. To start with, they had the best pictures and posters, with lean, camofaced, hatchet-wielding, badass looking guys. Their guns always looked light in their hands, and their kits looked like they were part of their bodies. I had read a book about Rangers while I was in Airborne School. It told me a lot, but only so much. They were, well, inscrutable as an organization. They called themselves the nation's direct-action raid force, but what did that mean?

Easy and I found ourselves in a classroom with a half-dozen other soldiers waiting for something, but not sure what it was going to be. Then two tall, lean Army staff sergeants walked in. They didn't say much; they just put on a video. Most of the video was filmed using night vision devices and was a bit hard to see, but we were pretty sure we saw men jumping out of airplanes with dirt bikes. That got our attention! When the film ended and the lights came back on, one of the staff sergeants began his well-polished briefing.

It was short and to the point. "Men, we want you to think about becoming Rangers. If you decide to try to become Rangers, you will be assessed during a mentally exhausting and physically grueling thirty-day indoctrination program. When you graduate, you will be assigned to a Ranger Battalion and deployed to Iraq or Afghanistan. What are your questions?"

Well, that was pretty abrupt! Some of the others asked questions while I processed what I had just heard. Then I couldn't help myself. I raised my hand and said, "Staff Sergeant, is it worth it? I mean the dangerous training and then the intense—and seemingly endless—deployments?"

I was ready for him to give me a long explanation of why becoming a Ranger was better than what I was going to be doing in the Army, but he didn't do that. He just said, "Do you want to be the best?"

I did, and compared with all the other options, I knew if I joined the Rangers I would get to the fight faster and would go into combat with the best men I could keep up with. I was ready to test my mettle and steel myself for the intense storm I imagined combat would be. Becoming a Ranger meant *hard*, but it also meant *fast*. I knew if I made it through Ranger training, I could be in Afghanistan fast-roping out of a helicopter with a machine gun before Christmas. Not to mention the dirt bikes!

The Ranger Indoctrination Program was demanding; it was the most challenging test I've ever faced. Army basic training had been demanding, and Jump School had been much tougher than that, but Ranger training pushed me to the limits. I know that many military memoirs—especially those by special operators like me—talk a lot about training. I won't talk about that in this book. One reason is that my main goal is to tell you what it was like to be part of the U.S. military's direct-action force in *combat* in Iraq and Afghanistan. The other reason is that the story of Ranger training has already been told well in Dick Couch's book *Sua Sponte*.

I graduated from Ranger training, received my tan beret, and became part of the 75th Ranger Regiment, 3rd Ranger Battalion. I was on the ground in Afghanistan fighting on December 28, 2006. Over the next six years I did six rotations to Afghanistan. I saw so many of my close comrades die on what can only be called suicide missions that I can't count—let alone name—them all here.

I could have made being a Ranger my career, but I received a medical discharge because of degenerative disc disease. I know that sounds like an old-person's ailment, but it happens to Rangers far too often. I had herniated a disk when I was a mortarman during my second deployment. I was young and strong, and "Ranger medicine" was a bit different back then. I stubbornly continued training and deploying.

By the time we deployed with Team Merrill in 2011, I knew I was living on borrowed time. Multiple herniations led to degenerative disc disease. Said another way, my body had been given a beatdown. Six deployments in six years had left me pretty banged up, and the Army did the honorable thing and medically retired me.

I'd been out of the Army for about two months when my friend Nicholas Irving said to me: "Paul, I had some tough missions as a Ranger, but I got out before it all hit the fan in 2011. I'm writing two books about my time as a Ranger sniper. You need to write a book about what you did, especially all the amazing stuff you did with Team Merrill."

I had served with Nick in Afghanistan in 2009. Nick was kind enough to write the Foreword for this book, and that should tell you something about how close we are. Nick has the well-earned reputation of being the deadliest Ranger sniper ever, with more than three dozen confirmed kills. (Nick wrote about his time as a Ranger sniper in two books, *The Reaper* and *Way of the Reaper*.) I know about many of these kills because I worked with him with my squad of Afghan Provisional Army. I hadn't read Nick's first book (the second one hadn't been published yet), and writing a book was the furthest thing from my mind.

But the more I thought about it, the more I decided that the Team Merrill story did need to be told, as well as the larger story of what had intrigued me as I did my research before joining the Rangers: Just what did "the nation's direct-action raid force" do for our country? I wanted to tell that story today, not wait decades before some historian or journalist decided to tell it. Not that I have anything against either of those professions—they do good work, but they didn't have the first-person experience I did.

Nick continued to challenge me to write this book, telling me, "You need to tell this story. People need to hear how leaving a war is so much harder than getting into one."

I knew immediately what he was talking about. In 2011 it was left to the 75th Ranger Regiment to "set the conditions" for our drawdown in Afghanistan. That's a politically correct way of saying we had to kill the terrorist leaders who would take over the country after we left. Otherwise, over a decade of Americans and our allies fighting and dying in Afghanistan would have been for nothing. But that mission was made all the more difficult because this was a time when Afghanistan was transitioning from military to civilian authority, and also a time when our ROE (rules of engagement) became so incredibly restrictive. You'll learn more about these ROE later.

So with all those military memoirs out there, why should you read this book? Let me explain it this way. Years ago, there was a popular car commercial that showed salesmen asking their manager how hard they should push and how many incentives they could give to sell cars. The manager replied, "Do whatever it takes." The meaning was clear: they *needed* to sell cars.

In 2011, Afghanistan was, far and away, America's longest war. The United States *needed* to get out of Afghanistan, and to do it with honor. As I said earlier, that couldn't happen with terrorist leaders ready to take over the country once we left. But wiping them out meant sending the 75th Ranger Regiment on high-risk missions day after day and night after night.

This is why I'm telling this story. General William Tecumseh Sherman famously said, "War is hell." Hunting down these terrorists, whose single organizing impulse was to kill us, was hell. But we did it because that's what Rangers do. In these pages, I'll take you to the hell that was Afghanistan in 2011.

WHEN
THE
KILLER
MAN
COMES

1

CHECHEN SNIPER

By the spring of 2011, the war in Afghanistan had been going on for a decade, and the United States was trying to salvage what it could from what was now our longest war. It was early in our seven-month deployment to Afghanistan. Our Ranger unit, Task Force Merrill, was based at Kandahar Airfield, the U.S. and allied operating base just outside of that city. Late one afternoon, our task force leader, Major Dan, told us to saddle up and that we'd be launching on a mission that night. We were going to launch out of Kandahar with the Night Stalkers of the 160th SOAR (Special Operations Aviation Regiment) and head for the Musa Qala District in Helmand Province.

Those Army Special Operations CH-47G Chinooks are flown by some of the most courageous pilots in the Army. They had taken us into hostile territory, and gotten us out, time and time again, knowing that at any time an enemy with an RPG (rocket-propelled grenade) could blow their helo out of the air. We trusted them, and they trusted us, and we'd rather work with them than with any other unit in any other service. In fact, while there are sometimes rivalries between various U.S. military units, there was no rivalry between the 75th Ranger Regiment and the 160th SOAR, only a solid bond. You could think of us as two sides of the same coin, we were that close.

We were briefed that our mission was to clear enemy fighters out of several villages in the Musa Qala District. We had good intel that the village was a stronghold and sanctuary for foreign fighters operating in southern Helmand, Sangin, and the surrounding areas. Past efforts to clear the area of these fighters had met with extremely heavy resistance, and the Musa Qala District was now believed to be an important command and control node where the Taliban operated with near-impunity.

For anyone who wasn't in the fight in Afghanistan, you can think of the Musa Qala District, and most of Helmand, the way you'd think of a Mafia-controlled neighborhood, or a pirate hideout in the Tortugas. It's a crossroads for bad actors where the Taliban, the Haqqani Network (an Afghan guerilla insurgent group), and foreign fighters wanting to join the jihad meet up. It's probably the worst den of iniquity in all of Afghanistan. Putting it mildly, there was overwhelming circumstantial evidence that there were high-value targets in the Musa Qala District that needed to be taken out.

While our intel was good, it wasn't perfect, and it

wasn't solid enough to send in conventional forces. So the decision was made to send in the Rangers—in force. At about 2200, 160th Special Operations Aviation Regiment CH-47G Chinooks loaded with us and all our heavy weapons lifted out of Kandahar Airfield headed for our objective area, close to several villages in the Musa Qala District. Two Chinooks carried 1st Platoon, Alpha Company, our sister platoon, and the other two carried 2nd Platoon, Alpha Company, the platoon I was with.

Some people think that special operators get pumped up before a mission, and they envision a bunch of guys getting fired up like a football team in a locker room. But it's not that way at all. As we settled into the Chinooks, each of us had our game face on and sat there silently reviewing the intel and going over in our minds how we were going to execute the mission. We each reached back to previous missions and thought about how we would deal with the unexpected—those things we hadn't planned for. If we knew one thing, it was that there was always going to be the unexpected—our enemy was going to get a vote.

One of my Ranger buddies who was from New York City told me that seeing us sitting on the hard canvas seats in a Chinook heading for a mission reminded him of the New York City subway. No one spoke, and there wasn't even any eye contact. There was only eerie silence as we each prepared for our mission in our own way.

Our intel told us we'd be going up against a ruthless, well-entrenched, and extremely well-armed enemy, so we were loaded for bear with two full platoons—about forty Rangers total—and all our heavy weapons. That meant we were carrying six M240 machine guns, six M249 SAWs (Squad Automatic Weapons), two 60-mm mortars, and two RAWS (Ranger Anti-Tank Weapons Systems), which were 84-mm antitank recoilless rifles. We had our personal weapons, mainly M4s, and, for several of us, our sniper rifles. I was cradling my M110 sniper rifle, which I had nicknamed "Miss America."

It wasn't a long flight from KAF to our objective area in the Qala District of Helmand Province. The 160th's Chinooks made short work of the 150 klicks (kilometers), about 100 miles, to our target. As we approached the objective area, the Chinooks carrying 1st Platoon broke off to the south to deliver them about 5 klicks from where we would meet at our proposed ROD (Remain Over Day) site. The Chinooks carrying our platoon, 2nd, broke off and landed about 10 klicks away to the south.

As soon as we landed, our platoon began to work our way toward the objective area along a dried-up riverbed, clearing small clusters of villages along its banks. ("Clearing" means making sure there are no enemies among the civilians.) In the hours we advanced, we cleared about one hundred houses, as well as countless other structures. If we found Taliban, or any other insurgents, our mission was to capture or kill them.

Major Dan's plan was clear: If we found nothing, we were to tell the villagers where we were going, knowing that they would alert the Taliban. I mistakenly took this as bravado, but in retrospect I realized it was exactly why we were on this mission.

From there, the plan was to remain over the day in a defensive position between the area we cleared and the northeastern outskirts of a much larger village. We would fight the Taliban there, or we would wait until nightfall before we started our infiltration.

The way that Ranger platoons work together is unlike any other U.S. Special Operations groups. When we execute a mission, we always share roles. In this case, we divided the labor between the Main Effort or the Assault Platoon and the Support Platoon.

The ROD platoon might conduct a quick takedown of a compound on its way to the ROD site, but its primary task was to fortify the compound where we intended to Remain Over Day. Said another way, the ROD platoon "provides the castle" for the Assault Platoon. They also carry the "Speedballs," which are bags containing extra ammo, water, food, and other gear carried on flexible litters. These Speedballs weigh several hundred pounds each, and humping them into a compound is a brutal task.

Once the ROD platoon had built the castle and given them a secure base to operate from, the Assault Platoon would conduct what we call a "clearance in zone" and investigate an NAI (known area of interest). You don't have to know a whole lot about Rangers to guess that being in the Assault Platoon was always first choice for all of us.

But it wasn't about doing what you wanted to do. Our 1st and 2nd Platoons alternated duties on each mission, sometimes attaching a squad or certain special weapons to one or the other, depending on the mission. It's a well-choreographed dance that we practiced dozens of times in our training cycle, and it gave us the ability to have the maximum flexibility in our infantry operations.

That meant we could go from small reconnaissance elements and "kill squads" to a full-on infantry company with a full complement of weapons, including a half-dozen 240s and 249s, several 60-mm mortars, and two sniper teams with a wide variety of sniper weapons. These included everything from the M110 to the SR-25 to the Barrett M2 to the Mk-13. A company-size element could form four sniper teams with what we call Squad Designated Marksmen, and could also have some K-9s (multipurpose canine teams).

On this mission, 1st Platoon was the ROD, or support platoon, so they made their way through a small village to the south of our proposed ROD site. Their objective was to clear and fortify that site and give us a secure area to operate from. On their way, they were ordered to conduct a raid on a compound that had drawn attention from Special Operations intelligence.

The raid site turned out to be a dry hole—something that would happen frequently during our deployment. First Platoon arrived at our ROD objective area around midnight and found an adobe house that was isolated from the surrounding villages. It was on low ground and was surrounded on three sides by high ground and on the fourth side by a large village that we hadn't cleared yet.

Our only ways out of this position would be back the way we came or through congested roads going through those villages.

But from a tactical standpoint, 1st Platoon had picked a good—even optimal—ROD position. We were about 500 meters from those villages and about 600 to 800 meters from the cliffs. With that kind of standoff from potential enemy fighters, it would be difficult for them to overrun our position. But the downside was that it would be equally difficult to defend long-range attacks from enemy RPGs or machine guns.

As was the case with most Ranger missions, there is no such thing as a perfect plan. Our mission was to draw the Taliban into attacking us, and if we wanted a fight, this position was as good as we could hope for, given the area and the terrain. After an animated discussion with the family that inhabited the house, including extended negotiations over how much they wanted to be paid to pack up and leave their home, they finally gathered a few of their belongings. But before they left, the 1st Platoon leader ensured his interpreter conveyed to the family that they were to tell everyone—especially Taliban—exactly where we were.

Meanwhile, our platoon—2nd, led by Major Dan—was the Assault Platoon, and we were making our way along the dried-up riverbed, clearing all the villages we passed through. This was our usual tactic, making sure we didn't leave any enemy fighters behind us in our haste to get to the objective area. Our predecessors had paid an enormous price in blood when they were ambushed from behind after not securing the area they passed through. We were humping all that heavy gear about, and even at night the Afghan heat was stifling. The thousand-plus-meter altitude made things just that much more of a slog.

We arrived at our objective area about 0330 and were met by 1st Platoon, who simply said, "Welcome to your new home." We saw immediately why they had picked this as our new casa. It was a typical Afghan dwelling—adobe brick walls about a foot thick and pretty nondescript, but large enough to house our two platoons. The house itself was two stories, with the second story offering a clear field of view for 360 degrees. The house was surrounded by a wall that was maybe two feet thick. Adjacent to the house, on its southern side, were the remains of what had once been another house, and that one was also surrounded by a wall.

We were exhausted from our trek getting to the ROD site, but no one could bed down yet. We surveyed the landscape around us through our NODs (night optical/observation devices). There were steep hills to the north, cliffs immediately to the east, a large village to the southeast, what looked like rock outcroppings and caves due south, a village to the southwest, and another village due west. We had intel telling us that the village to the west was a known area of interest where Taliban might be hiding, so 1st Platoon had cleared that village before we got there. They didn't find any Taliban—another dry hole.

Our platoon leaders assessed the threat from each of

those sectors and, armed with that info, we knocked holes in the adobe walls surrounding our outpost and positioned our M240 machine guns, M249 SAWs, 60-mm mortars, and 84-mm RAWS where we thought they'd have the best field of fire to deal with the potential threats surrounding us. Major Dan had 1st Platoon set up in the intact house, and our platoon, 2nd, set up south of them, in the rubble that was once a house. That meant that 1st Platoon would be responsible for a field of fire north from nine o'clock to three o'clock, while our platoon would have a field of fire south from three o'clock to nine o'clock. Our platoon leaders made guard assignments for the night and posted the first round of guards, and the rest of us finally grabbed a few hours of sleep.

It was early morning when about twenty elders came out of the village to our southwest and began approaching our outpost. At the same time, women and children in the village were moving in the opposite direction in a mass exodus—not a good sign. This had "ambush" written all over it. Despite the clear danger, Major Dan decided we needed to walk out of our compound and talk to the elders. I jumped at the chance to be part of the greeting party, all of us volunteers.

Major Dan, John, Ryan, "Stryker," our JTAC (Joint Tactical Air Controller), our Afghan interpreter "Zeke," and I left the mud walls of the compound where we'd camped out and headed toward the elders.

I knew, tactically speaking, that what we were doing was wrong. We were walking out onto low open ground.

Our relaxed posture was meant to show our goodwill toward the hopefully friendly elders, who could tell us if any Taliban were in the village. We were carrying our basic Ranger infantry weapons, our M4 rifles, and, for me, my M110 sniper rifle, Miss America.

That part of the plan worked—up to a point. The old men from the village walked toward us. They were trying to draw us into an ambush, and we were going to let them. This was a calculated risk, and we were counting on our fellow Rangers still inside the compound to provide over-watch and take out any enemy—especially snipers—who might threaten us. We knew our guys were scanning every-where, memorizing distances to likely targets, and making a mental map almost as fast as they could think.

Ryan and I hung back a few meters to provide cover-ing fire while Major Dan, John, Stryker, and Zeke met with the elders. They started questioning the men and patting them down, looking for concealed weapons. Ryan and I had worked together long enough that I could read my own anticipation in his posture: muscles loose, a relaxed grip on his M4, and breathing deeply to control the rising adrenaline.

We automatically scanned the elders as they were questioned by Major Dan through our interpreter, Zeke, and frisked by John. I was glad our commanding officer was leading the questioning. He was the one with the most experience in-country and had lived through Operation Rock Avalanche, hunting down Taliban fighters in the

Korengal Valley back in 2007. If there was anyone who wasn't going to be bluffed by the enemy, it was him.

Unlike many countries where our military operates, and where there is one language that we can learn in order to communicate with the locals, there isn't a single Afghan language. Instead, it's a multilingual country, with Pashto and Dari the dominant languages, but with many people speaking different dialects, such as Uzbek, Turkmen, Balochi, and Pashayi.

All this is by way of saying that for the U.S. military in Afghanistan—and especially for the Rangers in our role as a direct-action force that goes deep in-country to root out the enemy in villages and hamlets—an Afghan interpreter is worth his weight in gold. And Zeke was one of the best. He was an Afghan citizen who was embedded with us because he couldn't stomach what the Taliban was doing to his country. It was a life-changing decision, because once he had thrown in with us, he was a dead man walking if the Taliban caught him. It's hard for us in the United States to understand how brave these Afghan interpreters are, and we need to do more for them after they dedicate their lives to supporting us.

Major Dan and the others were engrossed in their task of trying to ferret out useful information about the Taliban from these old men, so Ryan and I scanned them, looking for suicide vests, concealed weapons, radios, or even just a suspicious gesture—anything to tip us off about what their real intentions might be. I was hoping that one would give himself away, producing a weapon or, worse, a suicide vest. None of them did—their lucky day.

Ryan broke the uneasy silence.

"Guy on the left, by the JTAC?" he began in a questioning way, wanting my input on whether that elder was a threat.

"He's okay," I began. "I'm looking long," I continued. Looking long means I'm in my sniper scope and my peripheral vision is reduced to zero.

"I've got the near sector," Ryan replied, unnecessarily. I trusted the big man implicitly, and he focused his attention on the elders and our greeting party.

One of the main tasks of a Ranger sniper is to be a counter-sniper. I continued to look long and scan the almost-white adobe buildings, with their seemingly random portholes and windows, where the elders came from. I saw a colorful drape blowing in one window, which could be an amateur's attempt at screening himself from view. I turned up the power of my scope, narrowing my view even more, until I could see into the room as if I were standing in it. There was nothing there, so I kept scanning.

"Anyone left in the village?" Ryan asked.

"Not that I can see," I replied. "Bad spot for a sniper, too."

"Maybe their sniper is as bad at his job as you are," Ryan jabbed back. I didn't look at him, but I could picture his wry grin and didn't bother with a response.

I opened my nondominant eye and took a knee, refocusing on the village elders, who were now shifting anxiously and glancing at the surrounding cliffs and mountains.

"Something on the high ground," I said to myself as much as to Ryan, as I shifted my scanning to the high ground.

"Where?" Ryan asked.

I nodded in the direction of where I had seen the elders looking over our shoulders.

"Look," Ryan said.

I didn't have to. He was pointing to the elders as one of them turned and began running away.

"Here we go," Ryan said.

I let out a short exhale of agreement that emptied my lungs. It was about to hit the fan, and my training kicked in. I began to focus on the basics of what snipers do. I started monitoring my breathing: *in, out, in, out*, I kept thinking, fighting to stay calm.

"Damn," I replied.

"There go the rest of them," Ryan said, disgust in his voice.

Time slowed to a crawl and the adrenaline began seeping into our bloodstreams. We hung back for four, maybe five heartbeats. Then all hell broke loose.

The morning calm was shattered by the unmistakable sound of AK-47 rifles and PRK-670 light machine guns—typical Taliban weapons. Their cyclic clack, clack, clack ripped through the air, echoing off the cliffs and mountains.

Instinctively, our seven-man greeting party hit the

dirt as enemy rounds exploded all around us. There was no cover where we were, and Ryan and I just hugged the ground and hoped dirt was the only thing the enemy hit. Major Dan and the rest of the team who had been questioning the village elders bounded past us, stopping just short of the wall of the compound. At the same time, Ryan and I were searching for targets, doing what we could to cover the greeting party's retreat.

Immediately, the Rangers in our house behind us broke their silence, and we heard the comforting *pop-pop-pop* of M4 carbines. The M4 is a shorter and lighter variant of the M16A2 assault rifle and is one of the Ranger weapons of choice.

As part of our fighting doctrine, as soon as a Ranger element takes enemy fire, every man in the unit can fire back with his personal weapons. But for heavier weapons, our weapons squad leaders or gun team leaders have to make the call.

I could pick out the deliberate snap of the M110 sniper rifle as Mac and his sniper team picked targets from their hide site in the cupola on the second story of the house behind us. Major Dan and his greeting party had made it back inside the compound, and now Ryan and I were running back to the cover of the compound walls. I stole a glance at Mac's position, jealous that he had the better vantage point. I saw a single round impact the wall behind me, and another sound pricked my ear.

Mac's probably taking Taliban heads off, I thought.

I saw a single round impact the facing wall of Mac's

hide site and a singular sound pricked my ear the same instant. The sound was too pronounced to be an AK-47. I figured it had to be a heavy machine gun—the sound it made was the *ka-chunk* that a machine gun makes after it fires a single round and then malfunctions. That told me that Mac and his hide-site crew were under the guns of the enemy.

The enemy fire was a booming counterpoint to the whisper of Mac's suppressed M110 sniper rifle. Mac and his sniper team were searching for the enemy who was ranging us, while the rest of the 1st and 2nd Platoon Rangers directed their fire at the enemy surrounding us on three sides. In no time, we could hear the Ranger gun team leaders yelling fire commands. We could picture the squad leaders shifting their teams to concealed gun ports they'd constructed the night before to concentrate their firepower. Soon we were beginning to return fire with the crew-served guns our weapons squad had brought to the fight.

Even in the heat of battle, we were able to assess and analyze. The Afghan Taliban are fierce fighters and worthy adversaries, and they have unmistakable fingerprints. With rare exceptions, they use AK-47 rifles, PRK-670 machine guns, and RPGs. The AK-47 has a distinctive pop, while the PRK-670 belt-fed machine gun has a characteristic grind that's unlike any other weapon. If the RPG is fired from a long distance, you won't hear the *whoosh* it makes as it leaves the launcher, but you'll see the distinctive smoke trail it leaves.

The good news is we knew what to listen for, but the

bad news was we were getting lit up by the enemy over an arc of almost 180 degrees. We heard the pop of the AK-47s and the grind of the PRK-670s from the cliffs immediately to the east, from the large village to the southeast, and from the rock outcroppings and caves due south. This was a well-planned ambush by a clever and heavily armed adversary.

Inviting the Taliban to a gunfight in an operating area heavy with enemy forces that was usually the responsibility of a Marine battalion hadn't seemed like a great idea back at KAF, and it sure as hell looked like a worse one now. Things were going to hell as our plan unraveled, and I knew our two platoons were now the hunted, not the hunters.

Suddenly, that distinct sound I had heard earlier caught my attention again, and I realized that what I had thought was a malfunctioning machine gun was actually a single large-caliber rifle round. I tried to time the crack of the bullet in supersonic flight with the bang of the powder burned at the rifle to give me a sense of how far away the shooter was. But I couldn't make out a bang. I had hoped that meant the enemy gun had malfunctioned, but sadly this wasn't the case. Another round impacted the cupola, and I made out both the crack and the bang. An enemy sniper was targeting us.

I thought I knew where the enemy sniper was—in the group of buildings to our southeast. But before I could key my radio to warn Mac and his team, I saw a trail of soot snake and bob directly toward their hide site. It was an

RPG, and it detonated, harmlessly, 15 feet from the wall. It was coming from the same area as the sniper—a typical Taliban tactic. I remember thinking, *Shit, Mac is really screwed.*

An enemy sniper, using his sniper scope, can make his partner with an RPG much more effective. We figured these guys weren't precisely co-located—that would compromise the sniper's hide site—but were within maybe 10 or 20 meters of each other, close enough that the sniper could yell to his RPG guy and tell him how to adjust his fire. It was a deadly combination. I knew that it wouldn't take the enemy long to figure out that he only had to move a bit closer to us, and his next RPG shot would hit the cupola and Mac and Hank, and our machine gun team would die.

By now, there was no finesse, either by the enemy or by us. What was the staccato of individual rifles or carbines firing deliberately quickly turned into a Ranger Death Blossom as our M240 machine guns and M249 SAWs opened up on the enemy in full cyclic firing. ("Cyclic" means a machine gun fires as fast as it can be fed bullets, so your only limitation is mechanical). Our platoon leaders went from one firing position to the other, directing our fire either at the cliffs, the village, or the rock outcroppings.

Having two Ranger platoons go full out in perfectly choreographed precision with every weapon they had was something beautiful to hear. Even our 60-mm mortars added to the noise and the uproar. The mortars couldn't be used to shoot the structures in the villages, where many of the enemy fighters were firing from, but they hammered the enemy's cave bunkers as well as the open ground at the edge of the villages.

I scrambled back into the compound. I knew I could help confuse the enemy sniper by picking a different position than where Mac and his spotter, Hank, were firing from. I found a good spot at the southeast corner of the southern compound wall and set up shop. I didn't have a spotter, but I knew Hank and his spotter had 16× optics, and they could radio positioning info to me. My usual spotter, Marc, was up in the hide site with Mac and Hank and couldn't get to me—he'd be exposed to the enemy sniper if he did and would never make it.

Suddenly there was a huge explosion. My MBITR radio came alive. (This is the AN/PRC-148 Multiband Inter/ Intra Team Radio, and it's pronounced "embitter.")

It was Mac. "Sierra, what the fuck was that?"

"Mac, Sierra, RPG," I said breathlessly. "Your hide site is compromised. If they have another RPG, you guys are fucked." I kept one eye on Mac's hide site as I adjusted my firing position.

"Roger, I thought it was an RPG. What did it hit?"

Mac wasn't getting it. "It didn't hit anything," I replied. "It just exploded. But we probably won't be as lucky next time. If these guys advance just a few meters they've got you nailed."

Before I could key my radio again and let Mac know that his position might be in the crosshairs of an enemy sniper, I heard three evenly timed sniper rounds tick into the front of the hide site like a metronome. Adobe dust poured from the holes in the building.

Good, I have a grouping, and none of those rounds killed anyone, I thought. Maybe I could locate the bastard who was trying to take us out.

"Go for the sniper!" Mac ordered. He knew that was the most immediate danger, and we both figured the enemy firing at us from a 180-degree arc were coordinating their efforts with their sniper, forcing us to keep our heads down while their sniper tried to take out Mac and Hank.

"Sierra, Mac, get eyes," Mac ordered. Mac sounded calm, but we both knew that an RPG hitting so close meant that his hide site and everyone in it was the enemy's primary target. A second RPG getting just a little bit closer meant they all died: three snipers and a machine gun team.

"Get eyes" is a sniper term for get to work. In this case, it meant get to a gun port and find a way to kill the enemy sniper. I shifted my position to the southeast corner of the compound and saw that our platoon leaders had moved two M240 heavy machine guns next to each other. Both were firing full cyclic, so I knew there must be something there.

I slid into the gun port next to one of the machine gunners, paralleled his barrel with mine, and looked down my sniper scope. I could see the impact of the machine gunner's rounds. He was firing at targets of opportunity, in this case an enemy adjacent to the enemy sniper's position, in the vicinity of where the RPG had been fired from.

They were chewing up dirt and kicking up a small whirl-wind of dust. All of this was within 25 to 50 meters of the sniper's position. I started a search pattern and tried to find a target. Nothing.

Meanwhile, Mac's team continued to answer with their suppressed sniper fire, near silent and withering, trying to take out the enemy before the next RPG connected. From the timing and direction of the sniper's rounds and the RPG shots, we were now sure the sniper and the enemy who had the RPG were located in the same general area and were coordinating their fire. It was the worst-case scenario for us.

I called Mac. "I think I have the sniper's location!" Locating this guy was 90 percent of the solution. Once we found him, we knew we could take him out. We were damn good at that.

"I've got him too!" Mac replied. We were trying to be calm and let our training click in. Sniping and taking out an enemy isn't like close-quarters fighting, where you let your adrenaline take over. I've always thought of sniping as like being in the eye of a hurricane—everything around me is blowing apart, but I have to stay calm enough to do the math and convey what only our telescopic sights can detect.

Mac and I kept scanning and memorizing what we saw. The sniper's primary location was exactly where we thought it would be. We kept looking. We found his secondary location, and then his tertiary one. We were thinking in the first person: *Where would* I *hide? Where would* I *run to? When would* I *pop my head up?*

This sniper was one clever and elusive dude. I knew he was good because I couldn't see him. He was in a hide site like Mac's, only it was better, because his building was surrounded by other buildings. He was built back into a room, screened from view, no doubt sitting comfortably, waiting to take out the first one of us who showed himself. Not too many Afghan Taliban are experienced enough to shoot at us from the back of one room screened by another room. This guy was screened two or three times and probably had a curtain of some sort with just a tiny path for his bullet.

Mac and I began piecing together and analyzing our enemy. You might think that the last thing Rangers involved in a firefight would do is analyze anything, but we do. That's how you win and, frankly, how you stay alive. We agreed this guy definitely wasn't a local—he was too good. And that made us flash back to 2010 and Operation Strong Eagle, when Mac and I were called on to counter-sniper a Chechen. We didn't kill that guy, but he didn't kill us. When you hunt a man who can shoot you from a mile away and you live, that's a win.

It's an old military saying that knowing your enemy is the key to victory. That goes double—maybe triple—for snipers. There weren't that many Chechen snipers supporting the Taliban, and with as long a war as we were fighting, we could identify individual Chechen snipers by

how they operated. An inexperienced sniper—which probably accounted for all the Afghan snipers we faced—will
try new things, switching tactics multiple times during a
fighting season. But these Chechen snipers—most of whom
had been honing their skills since the First Chechen War
with Russia in 1994—each had a way of operating that
identified him as accurately as fingerprints or a retinal
scan. Every time we faced one of these Chechen snipers
and avoided getting killed or injured, it gave us more info
we could use the next time we faced him.

We quickly realized that this sniper was good enough
that he'd make damn sure we never saw him or any sign
of him. So he was likely a Chechen, just like the one we had
taken on during Strong Eagle. And he was smart.

"Chechen?" asked Mac. But it was less question than
statement.

"Damn right," I replied.

"See any muzzle flash, ever?"

"Nope."

"You think it's a seven-six-two?" Mac asked, referring
to an old but reliable Russian-made 7.62 × 54R round, similar to our .30 caliber, a popular American cartridge often
used by U.S. Special Operations forces.

"No question," I replied. Even in the heat of battle we
could make out the distinctive thud of that 7.62 round, a
dead giveaway that it came from a Russian surplus rifle.
That meant we were dealing with a foreign fighter, most
likely a Chechen.

"We're not going to take him out like this. We need to collapse that house on top of him!" Mac said, the frustration coming through in his voice.

"Same shit, different day," I agreed. Even with the noise of our fellow Rangers firing full cyclic, pumping out max firepower at our enemy with their M240 machine guns and M249 SAWs, I remembered our sniper instructor's grave warnings about counter-sniper operations. The problem was that if I could shoot him, he could shoot me right back. It was as if we had invisible lines drawn between each other. The first man to slip or make an error was as good as dead.

Mac and I agreed that if this guy wasn't in charge of this ambush, then he was the eyes and ears of our enemy. He was coordinating his sniper fire with the Taliban, who were ranging us with machine guns and RPGs, and he was having them rake us with machine-gun fire when he moved from one position to the other. We weren't going to take him out with our probing fire.

I called my platoon leader. "Captain, this guy has us pinned down. We need to take him out!"

"Have you seen him or his muzzle flashes?"

"That's a negative, but we know where he's hiding and can locate him within a few meters. We can hammer him with sniper shots or rake those buildings with machine-gun fire, or you can bring in the Kiowas!" I replied.

However I was as a Ranger, I was respectful of authority and tried to keep my cool when I talked with our captain.

But I felt that I needed to be as direct as possible to ensure that he understood that this lone enemy sniper was dominating the entire engagement.

"Wait," he replied. I knew that meant he was going to talk with Major Dan.

"Captain?" I said, raising my voice a few octaves. I wanted him to make the decision, and I wanted him to make it right now.

I admit that I was getting pretty animated and was "leading" my captain all I could. I knew this Chechen was a hard target who was going to pin us down and pick us off like ducks in a shooting gallery unless we took him out. If we pulverized his defenses, we could force him to move and maybe expose his position. Then it would be a fair fight.

If I'd had my pick of all the options to take him down, it would be the Kiowas. I'd seen the Bell OH-58 Kiowa Warriors in action before, hosing down targets with their M134 miniguns and taking out harder targets with their FIM-92 Stinger missiles, AGM-114 Hellfire missiles, and Hydra-70 rocket pods. Let the Kiowas spit out enough firepower and they could collapse the building down around this guy.

I wanted this guy dead and I wanted him dead now, or my buddies weren't going to make it. It seemed like forever before the captain replied, and it wasn't what I wanted to hear.

"Captain, this asshole is a pro. He's buried in that building, deep in his hide site."

"Roger, keep eyes on, out," he replied. That was that. Sometimes you get your fire mission; sometimes you get your hands tied. This decision had been made well above both our pay grades.

I knew it was useless to argue with my platoon leader. I understood the ROE as well as he did, and they were restrictive. The enemy knew our ROE, and they didn't have to be great strategists or tacticians to conceal themselves in a way that killed our ability to use some of our awesome firepower.

We had to follow the ROE to the letter of the law, even if it meant taking on a ruthless enemy with one hand tied behind our back. And truth be told, I knew deep down inside it was the right thing to do. If we didn't follow our ROE, then we were no better than the Taliban. Doing the right thing was damn hard, but at the end of the day I realized it was a strength, not a shortcoming.

This was a lesson that would repeat itself over the course of our seven months in Afghanistan. Our commanding officer, Major Dan, had laid it all out to us in stark terms as soon as we had shown up in-country, and what he said made sense. It might seem easy to bend the rules, bring in all the firepower we could, drop the building right on top of the Chechen sniper, and try to justify it all later. But it would mean we had let our desire for violent revenge and self-preservation make us no better than the enemy.

So for now it was a chess game: their sniper was trying to target us, and Mac and I were trying to target him. Given how well this Chechen was hidden, we didn't think we had much of a chance, but we weren't going to give up.

It was about 0900 and the firefight had died down a bit. The Taliban were probing, trying to drive a wedge and somehow cause us to withdraw. Every time they probed, our machine guns and SAWs opened up and pinned them down. As this was happening, our three- and four-man fire teams worked in concert to cut down any of the enemy who were exposed.

There was a bit more than 600 meters between us and the closest insurgents, making hits difficult and confirmation more so. Our fire earlier in the day had been so intense we figured they must be taking casualties, but we never saw them fall and their probing fire continued. They knew the range of our weapons, and we knew the range of theirs. And they were smart. They knew if they only advanced to the edge of their village and probed from there, we couldn't bring in air power to take them out, since there would be too much risk of collateral damage.

Meanwhile, our requests up the chain of command to bring in firepower to take out the sniper, as well as the other Taliban pouring fire on us, were being "considered," but we weren't optimistic we'd get the answers we wanted. So we waited and continued to fight. The fire from the enemy AK-47 rifles and PRK-670 light machine guns would get intense for a few minutes; we'd respond in kind with our M4s, M240 machine guns, and M249 SAWs; and then things would get quiet for a while. By midmorning things had really died down, and we figured the enemy was regrouping and likely repositioning.

They opened up on us again around midday and we

fired back, but the fire on both sides was becoming less and less effective as we sized each other up. We were playing a waiting game, but we knew we had an ace up our sleeve: we owned the night. I'll explain what I mean by that.

A few years ago, a secretary of the Army, John McHugh, made public a phrase we had previously kept private within U.S. military ranks. He said this in a public forum while visiting an Army laboratory that designs new NVDs (night-vision devices), and the phrase quickly entered into common usage. I can't say I welcome letting potential adversaries know *anything* about U.S. military capabilities, but in this case the enemy has known about it for years.

Our nation has invested heavily in these NVDs, which allow images to be produced in levels of light approaching total darkness. An early version of this technology was used in World War II, and the technology has improved by leaps and bounds.

Meanwhile, word came down our chain of command that there'd be no relaxation of the ROE. That meant that, at best, we'd fight these bastards to a draw. It also meant that the 160th SOAR would be lifting us out of the Musa Qala District sometime after dark—but not before we capitalized on owning the night.

We'd been battling the Taliban in Afghanistan for over a decade, and we knew their tactics pretty well, as they knew ours. They'd keep fighting us in the daytime but would make a controlled withdrawal once darkness fell and melt back into the villages and the countryside. We didn't have a large enough force to hunt them down as they fled into their home turf, and it was definitely unfriendly turf.

By early afternoon, I'd finally decided I wasn't doing much good roaming among our fighting holes, so I made my way up to our sniper's hide site. Hank, who was Mac's spotter, and Marc were first on the rest plan, and they climbed down from the roof to sleep in the house below us. We didn't give them a time hack as to when to relieve us. They were both experienced Ranger NCOs (non-commissioned officers), and they slept wearing their Secret Service–style earpieces and kept their radios on. If it hit the fan, they'd wake up and we'd all fight as a team.

Mac and I watched the space between our adversary's little town and a village farther in the distance. Throughout the day, enemy fighters would come out of the town or village and make their way toward us. We had our sniper rifles dialed in on the edge of the village. That distance was between 900 and 1,100 meters, and I spotted for Mac with Miss America's scope. Mac would shoot first, and then I would shoot his "correction." After I fired, he would shoot my correction.

I would fire while Mac was resetting. Resetting means he had to ride the recoil of his gun and settle back on target. By the time he was settled back on target, the impact of my round or its vapor trail would be visible in his scope. Then he simply measured the distance between the trace of my round and our intended target. That was his correction, and he basically just moved the spot in his scope where he saw impact over our intended target and fired. I timed my breathing and trigger squeeze after I heard his round. I had an instant to observe his trace or impact, and then I fired my correction, giving him just enough time to settle again and see my impact and trace. One of our drills was to practice this as fast as we could, over and over, until we sounded like a metronome. We had been shooting the same guns together for over a year now, sometimes every day for months on end. We knew each other's weapons as well as we knew our own.

The day dragged on, and the enemy continued to attack us at random intervals. The Chechen sniper would crack off a few rounds aimed at our cupola to keep our heads down, and then the rest of our Rangers would be on the receiving end of a rapid barrage of machine-gun fire. We were still catching some amateur fighters when they made the mistake of crossing open ground, but we had to make our shots count, and quickly, because the enemy sniper would answer with his own rounds. This guy was too damn good, and by now some of his rounds had made it through the window of our hide site.

If you've taken enough enemy fire, you get really attuned to how a bullet sounds. When a round hits an exterior wall, you hear a *smack* sound. But when a sniper puts a round through a window of your hide site, you hear a *zip* as it whistles past you, and then a *smack* as it hits the interior wall. Then you typically hear the soft sound of adobe dust falling from the wall where the shot hit. We were hearing plenty of *zip-smack*s, and it forced us to keep our heads down.

It doesn't matter how many firefights you've been in—effective sniper fire *inside* your hide site will rattle you to your core. It's especially unnerving when you realize that if you didn't have the restrictive ROE you were being forced to comply with, your 60mm mortars could rain high explosive death down on the enemy.

It was late in the afternoon, getting near evening, and the fighting had become sporadic, with long periods of quiet. Marc had come to the hide site to relieve me, and I could have gone down into the main house and caught some sleep, but I tucked myself into a corner of the hide site instead. I was completely exhausted, but it felt better to stay with my sniper buddies than to go below and sleep in the Afghan home. Hide sites and fighting positions felt a lot more like home than the strangeness of trying to sleep in a home surrounded by the possessions of people whose language, culture, and daily habits were so unfamiliar.

I had just dozed off when I was startled awake by the now familiar *zip-smack* of a sniper's round hitting our position, followed by a coordinated barrage of enemy machine-gun fire. Mac was crouched below the windowsill, protecting himself from enemy fire. The enemy machine-gun fire intensified and there were a few pops of M4's from our side, but we didn't bother answering with our own machine guns.

It was jarring getting fired on by the enemy's heavy weapons and not responding in kind, but we were going to need the ammo we had left to fight our way out of there come nightfall, and our enemy—those left alive—were smart enough not to expose themselves. When one of our machine gunners did fire during the day, the enemy sniper drew a bead on them.

Remarkably, none of our guys were hit, but we all knew it was dumb luck. It's hard to describe the frustration you feel when you know that you and your buddies are escaping death by feet—even inches—and you also know that you have four of your own snipers conducting counter-fire and that you have mortars and a specially designed RAWS, as well as on-call air support to rain death on this ruthless bastard who's trying to kill us.

Suddenly, a sniper round snuck through our window with a *zip-smack* and bored its way into the wall behind me, inches above my head. Fine Afghan adobe dust poured down my collar. That was it. I wasn't afraid of death, but I wasn't going to let myself be a sitting duck, either.

Major Dan had set up his command and control position just below our window. He was facing us, watching the bullets make little waterfalls of sand on the exterior wall of our position. I popped up, fully framed by the window, and yelled, "Hey, sir!" to get his attention. In my rattled state of mind, I thought this would convince him that we should quit relying on dumb luck to stay alive.

Major Dan stared at me in disbelief, which I took as an acknowledgment that he'd heard me. Now that I'd made myself a target, evenly timed enemy sniper rounds were snapping into the walls around me, just a foot or two away from my head, like hands moving around a clock.

"Sir, am I really supposed to sit here and get shot at all day, or can I kill this fucking guy?" The words just came out of me before I knew what I was saying.

But before you could say "insubordination," First Sergeant Hutch saved me.

"You're going to sit there and get shot at, Sierra. Get the fuck DOWN," he ordered.

"Roger that!" I replied angrily, as I moved back and down from the window.

Meanwhile, Mac was listening to his platoon's radio frequency, and they were discussing our exfil plan (for exfiltration, the Army term for pulling us out of there). That was no surprise, as we'd walked into a hornet's nest. Our simple plan to round up some Taliban had unraveled for the same reason many military operations fall apart: the enemy gets a vote. In this case, the enemy had us where they wanted us—able to crush them but prevented from doing so by hugely restrictive ROE.

"Balls, we're going into that village as soon as it's dark," Mac said. "Better go below and get some rest. Could be another long night." He used my old nickname from my time in the Mortar Platoon, but he didn't mention anything about the stunt I had just pulled.

"Good call, man," I said, and carried my kit, as well as Miss America, on tired bones down to where we had made makeshift sleeping areas inside the house. I was pretty sure I would be in a heap of trouble when we got back. Everyone knows you don't get to yell at your commanding officer in the heat of a battle. You might get away with it behind closed doors during an animated discussion, but it's not okay to do it in front of half of his company.

I was lucky that I hadn't lost my life a moment ago, and I'd be lucky if I had a career when we got back to Kandahar. I rolled these two things over and over in my mind, and as night fell on the Afghan moonscape, I finally sank into an inky, restless slumber.

After nightfall, we did a Reconnaissance-in-Force (an operation used to probe an enemy's disposition) to gather whatever intelligence we could. Our platoon, 2nd, went into the surrounding villages to see if any Taliban had stayed behind. As we expected, they'd all melted away. Mac and I had told our assault squad leaders where we were certain the Chechen sniper had holed up. Sure enough, they found $7.62 \times 54R$ shell casings, and the extractor marks looked like they came from the Russian-made Mosin-Nagant sniper rifle. Based on the enemy sniper's rate and accuracy of fire, the spread of his rounds, and the other back-of-the-envelope math we were able to do, we were now certain this guy was a Chechen sniper—and a damned experienced one at that.

An enemy sniper can be the most dangerous man on the battlefield. I say "can" because with less restrictive ROE we could easily take out a sniper with our own mortars or call in air support—anything from Kiowas to Apaches to A-10 "Warthogs" to AC-130 gunships. In this case, our ROE wouldn't let us use any of those tactics; it was just sniper against sniper. Counter-sniper is the most dangerous thing a sniper can do because all your special techniques are neutralized. The enemy knows everything you're doing. You're no longer invisible, and you're no longer far enough away to be out of range.

It boils down to how well you were trained, your skill at applying your training, and, in this case, your equipment. I knew full well that if I had had the Chechen's gun and he had had Miss America, I wouldn't be here to write this book. It's probably the most frustrating aspect of my entire rotation to Afghanistan. They say you fight the way you train. In the case of a Ranger sniper, I'm trained to call for close air support, and my equipment means I have an invisible line to that aircraft. Said another way, it's not just about being a sniper who can put a bullet somewhere specific. I'm an organic limb of the team. I'm the eyes for its machine guns. I can tell a commander where to put his mortar rounds. And perhaps most deadly to the enemy, I have a radio connected to Kiowas, Apaches, A-10s, AC-130 gunships, and other air support I'm not able to talk about here. Restrictive ROE takes all that away, and I'm just one dude with one rifle.

It took us several hours to clear the village, ensuring that there was no enemy hiding there, and then we walked to the southwest to reach our exfil site. I remember my legs feeling like lead. It was the first time in a long while when I felt like my tank was completely empty. It was a hard-earned lesson in pacing. The march was all but silent.

After an op like this, we didn't have much energy left for communicating. You're so tired that you become an Army robot. You just march. But while you do, you pull security, you triple-check every task, and you keep performing to standard.

Our 160th SOAR brothers lifted us out of there and back to KAF. We all were bone-weary from our Musa Qala District op and frankly a bit shaken by how good the enemy had been. We had known this rotation to Afghanistan wasn't going to be a cakewalk, and we now also knew we needed to reassess our enemy. I also knew that someone had to speak up about the ROE we were dealing with.

We mustered in our TOC (Tactical Operations Center) at KAF the next evening and sat down to do the AAR (After Action Review) of our mission. AARs are an important part of what we do, and we never skip them. It's all part of the learning process and how we up our game for the next mission.

During the AAR everyone was tense, and while we all kept the discussion professional, it was intense and often heated. We had a lot to say to our leadership about ROE, and all of it was negative. After the AAR, I asked to speak with my captain one-on-one. He agreed, and we stepped out into the hallway outside the TOC.

"What's up, Sergeant Martinez?" he began. He could tell I was angry, but he took it in stride. He knew you can't spell "Ranger" without "Anger," and he knew my anger wasn't directed at him.

We didn't have complete privacy. There were a lot of other Rangers coming and going around us, and we would stop talking when someone approached. My captain's tone was completely neutral, even accommodating, but in spite of my best efforts my tone was stern, even heated.

I started out carefully. "Sir, I think I need to explain to you what it is Mac and I and our boys have been trained to do." I began to list all the reasons why he needed to trust us to do exactly what our training enabled us to do.

"Captain, we told the assault squad leaders what buildings, by the numbers, the Chechen sniper was firing from. (We assign temporary consecutive numbers to each building on a mission to identify them.) Sure enough, they found $7.62 \times 54R$ shell casings with light extractor marks scattered all around. I'm sure you know that meant he was firing a Mosin-Nagant, like we said he was. We knew that because of the group size of the rounds impacting the wall of our cupola and because of his rate of fire. The bulk of the casings they found were at Building 33, his primary hide site."

"That was the building we called up for a fire mission. The same shell casings were also found at Building 15, which we called up as his secondary position. We knew he was inside those buildings, not outside, and we also knew that he wasn't hiding in the cliffs because of the sound of his report (the sound his rifle makes). Buildings 15 and 33 were the only ones where he would have had the right size loophole facing the right direction with cover for his egress.

Mac and I both agreed that those would be *our* first choices for a sniper hide."

My captain continued to listen, and this didn't surprise me. He was a good leader, and that's what good leaders do. I continued to pour out my story.

"We knew roughly how far away he was by his second or third round. We knew he wasn't an amateur because he coordinated his fire with his machine guns, and he chose his targets in the exact order of priority that *we* were trained to do. He fired at random intervals so that he could reduce his already minimal signature and keep us from timing his rounds for our own counter-sniper rounds. He picked out our hide site immediately; it was the first thing he shot at, even though we had spent hours before dawn concealing our presence there."

The captain was surprised we had so much SA (situational awareness) and said so. He had come up through the ranks—he had been an NCO before he was an officer— and he knew that my loud talking and anger venting weren't directed at him personally.

"Sir, there are only so many people who can do what that guy did today, and most of them work for us. We got really lucky—one more RPG and we would have had to bury half our snipers as well as our machine-gun team. If he had gotten a hundred or two hundred meters closer to us, his group size would have been the size of our fighting holes, not greater, and we would have taken a lot of casualties."

He paused a bit before replying. I could tell he was struggling with how to say what he was about to tell me. "I hear what you're saying, Sergeant Martinez, and I appreciate you coming to me with this. But we all know the ROE is what it is, and I can't change that. I get it, though. If you know what you say you do, just do what you know is right, and we'll back you up."

To be completely honest, I hadn't expected him to be so understanding. I finally began to realize that he was just as frustrated with the ROE as my buddies and I were. The Captain recognized my arguments had merit, and acknowledged the gray area we were operating in. I trusted my gut that I'd make the right decision, and now I realized that he trusted me as well. That didn't mean I had carte blanche to shoot whoever I pleased, but I felt like we had built some trust in the last 36 hours of intense combat. What I took away was that he trusted me enough to know that I *wasn't* going to shoot whoever I pleased. He promised to take my concerns up to Major Dan and said they'd discuss it with the other platoon leaders and platoon first sergeants.

I walked back to my CHU (containerized housing unit), which was nothing more than a small shipping container with two beds in it. On the one hand, I was relieved that my concerns would be brought up the chain of command and get a fair hearing; on the other, I was still frustrated that somewhere near the top of that chain, someone was still making us fight with one hand tied behind our back.

After that battle with the Chechen sniper, I still couldn't believe I was alive. I also couldn't believe that my first sergeant didn't chew my ass for yelling at Major Dan. But above all else, I couldn't believe we were going to fight like this for the rest of our rotation in Afghanistan.

2
NIGHT OPS

Not all of our missions with Team Merrill in Afghanistan were like our encounter with the Chechen sniper. That one was short-fused and based on emergent intelligence. While we "planned" the mission, it wasn't the deliberate planning we liked to do in order to enhance the chances of mission success.

The night mission described in this chapter fits the mold of a classic Ranger mission with deliberate—even methodical—planning. We knew it was a mission where owning the night was going to be crucial. The objective area was a small farming community in South Helmand Province, not far from Kandahar.

Our intelligence told us this town was under complete Taliban control. This meant that a shadow government was acting with the full support of the community, and that the Taliban controlling the town were taking orders from Taliban higher-ups operating from safe havens in Pakistan. This seemed a likely place for smuggling, caching of supplies, and safe-housing of foreign fighters.

Team Merrill was a fully manned unit, and many of us had been in the 75th Ranger Regiment for years. We had tight bonds—the kind that are formed in fire and tempered by what was shaping up to be a never-ending conflict. I had met and worked with most of the guys from Alpha Company. I had worked for 1st and 3rd Platoons, but I didn't have much more than first impressions of 2nd Platoon.

We spent a good bit of time in the early stages of the deployment sizing each other up. As I sat and listened to the extended mission briefing for this night operation, my thoughts drifted to the men sitting in the TOC with me. I would have to watch their backs and they would have to watch mine. My life and limbs were on the line, and to say that meant I had more than a passing interest in knowing each of them even better than I knew my own brother is an understatement.

"Knowing your brother" means something different to a Ranger. You'd think that people who spent months on end together would know each other the way college roommates do. In other words, you'd know things like their preferences in women, cars, sports, clothes, movies, and TV shows.

While we did talk about those kinds of things, we also knew each other on a completely different level. We did this because we *needed* to. We found common ground on levels that soldiers have for millennia. I wanted to know about each of my fellow Rangers at an intimate soldiering level, and I'm certain they wanted to know the same things about me. How do you get ready for a mission? How do you prepare your kit? What are your physical, mental, and emotional limits? What rattled you on previous missions? How do you work out to ensure you're at the top of your game?

We needed to find out things about each other that would enable us to have each other's backs in combat. Too many outside of our community think that all special forces operators are supermen. We're not. But we're all in it together, and without putting too fine a point on it, once we rotate in-country together, we're more or less stuck with each other. So each of us needs to know certain things. Who is decisive, and who less so? How fast can you run or walk if we're moving into, or out of, an objective area? Who is comfortable with a rigid plan, and who needs more flexibility? Who would freeze under fire, and who would fire back? Did I need to rein in a machine gunner or urge him on? Would someone carry his buddy on his back and never quit?

The thing was, even though you all had gone through the same selection and training process, you never knew how each of your brothers would perform under the pressure of combat—and you were frequently surprised. I served with Rangers who were former blue-chip college athletes who would fall out when trying to carry a casualty, while a guy who had never worked out before his Army service made the same casualty-carry look easy. You just didn't know, but you *needed* to know. And the most important question was this: Would you give your life for your buddy?

As I sat there in TOC with the men I was about to go into combat with, everything about the way this mission was shaping up made me flash back to a fight I'd been in the year before. On that mission I had sized up a totally different group of men—Navy SEALs who we would be fighting alongside—and their senior sniper, Senior Chief Petty Officer Thomas A. Ratzlaff, who insisted everyone just call him "Rat." The SEALs had our backs, and we had theirs. But I hoped to hell tonight's mission wasn't going to be as hairy as that one had been. My mind went back to that night mission in Nangarhar Province.

That fateful night in 2010, we (1st Platoon, Alpha Company, and a troop of SEALS climbed aboard our 160th SOAR Chinooks, launched out of JBAD (Jalalabad) at 2000, and flew to our FARP (Forward Air Refueling Point) site at FOB (Forward Operating Base) Laghman. We loaded up some more SEALs and finally arrived at our HLZ (Helicopter Landing Zone) around 2230. We set down in some fallow fields in a draw at the base of some giant mountains.

We slogged through the rough fields and onto what passed for a highway, heading for our objective area, about 10 klicks to the northeast. It was a small village, and our intelligence told us there were senior Taliban leaders who had taken control and were using it as a staging point for attacks throughout Nangarhar Province. This had danger written all over it, as we had flooded walled-in fields to our east and impenetrable mountains to our west. We had excellent night-vision devices, but they needed a bare minimum of light to be effective, and we had none. We were literally groping our way along what was little more than a goat path.

Mac was near the front of our combined Ranger/SEAL formation as we continued toward our objective area, beginning our climb to higher ground. I was pulling rear security as I watched the fuzzy silhouettes of Rangers and SEALs pick their way up the mountain. Once or twice during the ascent I heard the scrape of a man or equipment when one of us misjudged our path, but overall we were as silent as ghosts.

When we finally reached the ridgeline, we could see the target village lying in a small valley. The village was small—maybe a few hundred people—with only two or three electric lights glowing.

We picked our way along the ridgeline until our point man found the trail. It was barely wider than my feet side by side, but it was the best—and only—way down. Everything else was cliff or a scree. It was also the last place where the Taliban would expect us to attack.

As we made our way down the mountain, Mac and I split up so we could provide overwatch for the SEALs. We had good fields of fire that overlapped the entire village. Mac had a bit of high ground to the west of me. I hunted among the boulders and rubble that had sheared off the cliff face, looking for clear firing lanes and good cover.

It never failed: all the best shooting lanes had the worst cover. What that meant was I had to rely on the cover of darkness. The night would provide a thin layer of security, but one that would be compromised as soon as we started firing and the enemy saw our muzzle flashes.

As we continued to provide overwatch, the SEAL team moved into the village. They were able to conduct a surreptitious breach of a large compound in the middle of the village, quietly rounded up everyone in the multi-family dwelling, and did their tactical questioning. Then did the same thing in two more compounds.

The SEAL troop didn't find any persons of interest in the compounds, which happened frequently when we went on missions with imperfect intelligence. They began to make their way back to our lines at the bottom of the cliffs as our Ranger machine-gun teams broke down and followed, covering the SEAL troop's movement. It was a methodical withdrawal, since we knew that if there were Taliban in the village we would be outnumbered with our backs to the cliffs.

The last fire team of SEALs was making its short movement out of the village when suddenly we heard AK-47s popping off. The sound was coming from the northeastern edge of the village. The rounds weren't coming over our heads immediately, and I could hear that Mac was holding his fire. I moved to a small outbuilding and quickly climbed to the roof.

Then all hell broke loose. We started taking small-arms fire from various spots in the village. I went prone, willing my body to meld with the hard ground. One of the SEAL snipers was just to my left, and we both scanned the village looking for muzzle flashes. We couldn't see any, which told us the Taliban had ideal positions. It also told us we weren't in immediate danger—a *very* relative term when you're the target of a Taliban ambush. The mission had just gotten a lot harder.

I started to raise my head and try to get my gun into the fight when rounds snapped over my head and I knew the Taliban were ranging us. I quickly dropped my head to the ground and stayed prone as I tried to scan the village through my sniper scope.

The SEAL sniper to my left saw movement in the village about the same time I did.

"Hey, Ranger," he said. "Do you see that guy at Phase Line Broncos in the intersection?"

I knew where to look immediately. Our labeling scheme was to put a "phase line" over a road or some other landmark, and we tended to use the names of professional sports teams to label them. In this case, Phase Line Broncos was the main east-west road through the village, and my SEAL counterpart—and now teammate—was tracking the same motion I had just noticed.

I adjusted my aim just a bit to the left and zeroed in on a man in an intersection.

"I've got him at two hundred fifty meters, white dish-dash and brown pants," I replied, referring to the robe-like garment worn by Arab men sometimes called a dishdasha. I could see he had an AK-47 at his side.

"That's him," my SEAL partner replied excitedly. "He's got an AK."

No more words needed to be exchanged. I centered the man in my crosshairs, favoring his left side because of the wind I felt on my cheek. I took up all the slack in my trigger and broke a shot, and so did my SEAL partner.

We saw the man twitch, as one or both of our rounds passed through him, but he was still standing. We fired again, and this time our guns made a tick-tock rhythmic sound. Then I saw that the man was half-falling, half-clawing his way backward. I couldn't tell if he was dying, but in an instant he was out of view, obscured by the heavy foliage and winding adobe walls of the village.

"I think we got him!" my SEAL partner shouted.

I was amped up and answered loudly, "I think so, too. Scanning right!"

Celebrating isn't fighting, and his silence meant he was scanning left. We both knew our sectors would over-lap in the middle. The sun was now fully up, and I felt the giddy delirium that comes from the combination of physi-cal exhaustion, sleep deprivation, hunger, and adrenaline. Rangers are solar powered, and the dawn light always invigorated me.

We were still scanning the village, looking for addi-tional targets, when an enemy hand grenade burst to our left, about 50 meters west of us. My SEAL partner and I were well out of its lethal range, but that wasn't the case for the SEALs and Rangers making their way out of the village.

That also meant that unless Tom Brady had chucked that grenade, the Taliban were close enough to smell. The dense, forest-like canopy of orchard foliage completely concealed them from our elevated vantage point. And that was what worried me. There could be a dozen Taliban fighters, or there could be hundreds.

We couldn't see anyone in the dense foliage beneath us, so our priorities quickly shifted. We needed to make sure that the Taliban we couldn't see weren't reinforced by fighters in the village we could see. My SEAL partner and I turned our attention back to the right and scanned long.

I had line of sight to another intersection on Phase Line Broncos, and I could see men with what could only be guns flash through the narrow opening.

"I've got movement!" I shouted to my SEAL partner.

"Roger, I've got it," he replied.

I snapped off two or three rounds each time I saw the flash of a man, and my SEAL teammate did the same. Our shooting lane was so narrow that if we hit someone it was likely that their momentum would carry him out of our view, even if he was mortally wounded.

Suddenly an enemy hand grenade detonated just 15 to 20 meters in front of the building where I was perched. I could hear the sizzling shrapnel zip over my head like jagged red-hot buzz saws. I instinctively flattened myself on the roof, my cheek pressed into the dirt roof of the building. I was looking directly at the SEAL sniper, who was also doing his best flat-as-a-pancake impression.

"See anything?" I asked.

"Nope. You?" he replied. If we weren't both puckered up tighter than a knot on a balloon, we would have laughed.

I tipped my head up just a bit, and somewhere to the west I could hear Mac's M110 sniper rifle snapping out fast bursts of three or four rounds at a time. I could tell that he was going to work on the intersections and gaps, just as we were.

I looked forward and down at the mini-forest of fruit trees in front of me, and an unseen enemy sprayed his machine gun at us. His bursts arced just inches over our heads. I flattened myself again, frustrated that this guy had us ranged and that he was keeping me and Miss America from getting into the fight.

Meanwhile, all along our east-west phase line, Rangers and SEALs were picking off enemy fighters with disciplined precision. I snapped back into pancake position.

My SEAL sniper partner asked, "Do you see anything?"

I tried to force a laugh and managed a smile. We both knew this was preposterous. We may as well have been on a life raft surrounded by sharks in the middle of the ocean.

Suddenly more AK and machine-gun fire poured over our heads and into the walls of the outbuilding where we had what passed for cover. We were the definition of pinned down, out of moves, with Taliban 10 to 20 meters in front of us and nearly sheer cliffs behind us.

"Rock and a hard place," I groused to my SEAL partner.
"Damn right," he hissed. He looked as tense as I felt.

All we could do was hug dirt, listen to our MBITR
radio, and trust that we'd soon hear the Ranger Death
Blossom that would buy us some space. I wanted to hear
those M240 machine guns and M249 SAWs going full cyclic. I *needed* to hear them.

One of our team leaders was on the ground to my left
taking cover, such as it was, behind a boulder slightly
smaller than he was. A burst of machine gun fire hit the
boulder and the dirt around it, and I watched him press his
back to the rock and suck his elbows in. He slouched, buying some space.

I watched as he turned slightly, trying to bend around
the boulder to return fire in a near-prone position. A second later, he rolled back behind the rock as another burst
obliterated the rocks around him.

One of his privates, using our building as cover, sprayed
a full magazine back at the Taliban who was trying to kill
his team leader. He jumped behind the building, changed
out his magazine, and sprayed another full burst toward
the Taliban.

Our team leader, hearing the lull in enemy fire, started
firing from the position where he had almost died an instant ago. I heard American weapons kicking up their rate
of fire on my left and right.

The enemy was engaging us decisively now, closing in
with AK-47s and hand grenades, trying to dash us on the
cliffs that loomed behind us.

Our Rangers on the ground opened up with the Ranger Death Blossom, and SEALs piled on with all their weapons. The deafening, withering noise of heavy weapons finally blunted the Taliban advance, buying us time to exfil.

"All right, let's get everybody up and ready to move," our platoon sergeant called across the Radio Net. "First Squad, you're leading out. Start pushing up the mountain."

Each Radio call sign called back with just his call sign to confirm the order. Meanwhile, the SEALs used their own internal net to do the same thing and begin their exfil beside us.

We wasted no time gathering up our forces and began pushing up the mountain.

I was the person closest to the goat path that would lead us out, and Mac was passing the Line Infantry Rangers in a rush to get to me. Rat was behind him, moving with the fluid ease of someone who has spent over a decade in body armor and fighting kit.

"Balls, I'm going up toward the front, Mac said. "I'll call you when I have eyes; then you move."

Mac's plan made sense, and I nodded, happy to agree. He was going to push hard and fast up the mountain, find a good overwatch position, and cover us from there. I would be at the rear with Rat, and we would move under Mac's cover. Once we moved, we would cover Mac and the rest of our men as they continued up the mountain.

This meant that we would be the last ones in the fight. It was a dangerous honor, but it was a milestone for me to be trusted with the security of both Rangers and SEALs, my childhood heroes.

Rat and I divvied up our sectors and pointed out the places we wanted to climb to. We stuck close together, but not too close to the trail fire team. We had to make sure we weren't in the same RPG blast radius. We weren't going to make the Taliban's job easy. If they wanted to get us, they would have to do it one at a time.

My earpiece came alive again. It was Mac.

"Sierra up," he called out over the net breathlessly, meaning he had Rat and me covered.

I glanced over and gave Rat a slight nod. He reciprocated, and we moved out.

Suddenly, I heard a *snik* sound from Mac's rifle 100 feet above us. Rat and I didn't need any more encouragement to haul ass up the mountain.

We got to our planned positions, found a bit of cover among the boulders, and turned our attention back to the village. What I saw sent chills down my spine.

There were half a dozen heads poking around corners and flashes of men with rifles crossing small open spaces. We took rapid aim and shot fast, sacrificing accuracy for speed. We wanted to kill every one of those Taliban, but more than that, we needed to keep them from killing us and the rest of the Rangers and SEALs who were trying to get up the mountain and out of danger.

All we had were our sniper rifles and a handful of men turning back to discourage these guys, so we had too many targets to waste time trying to get the perfect shot.

I remembered something Mac had once told me: "Take the shot you have; make the shot you need." We needed the enemy to hesitate, to make mistakes, to be afraid, and to hide. If they got a machine gun up in a good firing position, they could effectively wipe us out.

We leap-frogged two more times, and when we were almost to the crest of the small pass, the enemy fire stopped completely. We relaxed for a moment, catching our breath as we moved over the relatively flat terrain of the ridgeline.

If the Taliban came at us now it would be suicide, and they knew it as well as we did. Mac was already near the bottom of the cliffs, which made a semicircle around us, and he moved north to cover the MSR (major supply route) on the east side of our HLZ exfil point.

"Balls, we need to cover that pass. And the southern approach of the MSR—what's it look like up there?" Mac asked, rather than just telling me to take the high ground.

That triggered something inside me. We were at the end of this rotation in Afghanistan, and this was the last mission we'd be on together, at least this year. I felt I must have proved something to Mac over the last four months and had earned his trust. He was one of the toughest team leaders in 3rd Ranger Battalion, and he was treating me as an equal.

"Looks good to me," I replied, with renewed confidence.

It wouldn't be easy, but I wasn't about to say so. I had proved myself once, and I wanted to do it again.

"Roger, break down at two mikes," Mac called back

casually. ("Mike" is slang for minute.) He meant for me to scramble down the mountain and make the HLZ in time to be the last man on the bird.

Rat was still beside me, and he was hearing the same thing on the SEALs' own frequency.

"Looks like you're coming with me," Rat said. He was as calm as if the firefight we had just survived had never happened. I just nodded and smiled back.

I was in disbelief that I was one helicopter ride away from surviving the bloodiest year in Afghanistan as a brand-new sniper. And the unanticipated, unbelievable bonus was that I got to do one last bit of hunting with a sniper from SEALs.

Rat and I picked our way along the trail, got to a spur on our edge of the ridgeline, and found good shooting positions where we could cover the rest of the exfil for our guys. We sat there the morning sun, looking at the green fields and the mountains reflecting the pink hues of the sunrise. We scanned and chatted but never said the obvious: that this mission almost got all of us killed.

Soon we heard the reassuring thump of the 160th SOAR Chinooks. We rushed down the mountain like deranged billy goats, boarded the birds, and headed back to Kandahar.

That mission where Rat and I had escaped by the skin of our teeth was firmly in my mind as I listened to the briefing for our mission that night and looked at each man in the TOC.

Staff Sergeant Mac was the one teammate I already knew well, since we had been partnered together on our last rotation to Afghanistan and had fought together in south Helmand Province before that. He had been the squad leader for our sniper section and the sniper team leader during our previous deployment. At the end of the day, Mac was the best NCO I ever worked for. He taught me everything I know about how to be a good Ranger.

Then there was my sniper teammate Marcus. Good ol' Marc. He was a squirrelly, red-haired Puerto Rican guy with high energy and a short attention span. He was always moving and always talking in his high-pitched, nasal voice. Marc was a kind of "Mr. Gadget" who was always looking at new guns and other gizmos to add to his kit. If he didn't have it, no one did.

Our officers were first-rate, the kind of men you would follow on any mission, even if you knew your odds of dying were too damn good. Major Dan was our company commander and probably the best officer I ever served with. He had been there and done that. He didn't talk down to us during briefings. He didn't even talk *to* us. He talked *with* us, inviting questions in such a way that you knew he really wanted to hear what you had to say. It was almost like we were playing a pickup football game and one guy—not the quarterback—came into the huddle with a good idea and we all went with it. And it wasn't because that guy had been given his authority by the coach, but because what he said just made a hell of a lot of sense.

Then there was my platoon commander. I'll just call

him "Captain" or "Cap." He wasn't a big man—maybe five-foot-ten—but he was built like a tank. Some people in leadership positions feel they have to project to be recognized as leaders. Cap wasn't like that. He was spare with his words, and when he said something during the mission briefing he conveyed it concisely and accurately. For all of us in Alpha Company, that meant that when he gave an order, you could trust it was the right thing to do.

My platoon sergeant, Sergeant Pack, was a study. He was small, maybe five-and-a-half feet at the outside. Small guys usually go one of two ways in the Rangers: either they get looked down on because they don't fit the Ranger mold, or they have a serious Napoleon complex and can't wait to get their first stripe so they can start bossing everyone else around.

Pack didn't fit either of these. He was tough but fair, and above all else we felt we could trust him. Platoon sergeants lead in a few different ways, and they are justifiably the baddest man in the platoon. Some of them leverage that toughness; others leverage their wisdom and proficiency. Sergeant First Class Pack led with his heart, and his decisions were tempered by an unwavering principle: that all of us should live through this and go home whole.

Staff Sergeant Bill was our Weapons Squad Leader. He was a big guy, over six feet tall and heavyset, and he gave off the aura of someone you didn't want to mess with. He was the ultimate by-the-book kind of guy. One of his key duties was to help integrate Alpha Company's augmentees, like snipers and mortarmen, since some of our own senior leaders were augmenting other Ranger strike forces.

Staff Sergeant Josh was another squared-away leader. He was pretty, too, something we didn't let him forget. Josh was tall and slim and looked like he'd been a swimmer or a runner in school. I found out later in the rotation that he was from California and was an avid surfer. That was probably why he was so laid back.

Sergeant Reggie was the biggest guy in the room, and he knew it. Standing out as the biggest guy in a Ranger company meant something. In Ranger units, if the biggest guy is also squared away, he becomes something of a team mascot. This goes back through centuries of fighting—at least as far back as the Middle Ages, when armies had a champion in the form of some huge brute. If we still fought with swords and shields, Reggie would be the guy we sent out to fight the other army's baddest dude.

I thought Staff Sergeant John was the most interesting guy in 2nd Platoon, and maybe the entire company. He was from New York City, had been there on 9/11, and was a true believer. He wanted to kill as many terrorists as fast as he could, and he wanted to keep doing it again and again. He had done a turn in HHC (Headquarters and Headquarters Company), my parent company, and we were fast friends.

It's one thing to be brave, and another to be well trained, but these Rangers I'd be going into the fight with were an experienced bunch. That gave me confidence that we'd be able to deal with whatever the enemy had to dish out. I mentally placed this group in the mission Rat and I had been on, and I felt we could have handled that one just as well.

The briefing complete, we grabbed our gear and humped it outside, then gathered on a concrete pad for FMC (Final Manifest Call). It was still an hour before dawn, and stepping out into the January cold in Kandahar—just a few degrees above freezing—shocked us out of the lethargy of an hours-long briefing inside our TOC. Our breath collected into a single small cloud over our heads while we checked our communications gear.

This mission was a single-platoon operation for 2nd Platoon. Our 1st Platoon had its own mission in another objective area it would be heading for. This was the most typical kind of Ranger op. We sometimes went on a mission as an entire company, as we did on that operation in the Musa Qala District. But more often the nature of the mission called for a smaller footprint, and a single Ranger Platoon—about two dozen men—was the right force to get the job done.

This was my first mission as sniper team leader. Marc and I had rehearsed our plan as best we could. For Rangers, it's not just about fighting; there's a hell of a lot of planning and briefing—and, when there's enough time—rehearsal. That means we're doing all we can to ensure mission success, and frankly, it saves lives. Special Operators live by the motto, "Hope for the best, but plan for the worst," and we planned for every contingency we could think of.

It wasn't officially fighting season yet; that wouldn't come for another month or two. Although the term "fighting season" is used on the television news or in the newspapers, few civilians really understand what it means.

Afghanistan is a mountainous country, and in the wintertime the mountain passes that are the normal transit routes throughout the country—and especially between Afghanistan and Pakistan, where the Taliban have many of their safe areas—are impassable. So during the winter, from about late October to early March, the Taliban typically hunker down and don't conduct any major operations.

Even though it wasn't fighting season, the Taliban had already infiltrated and even taken control of numerous villages in the region. This meant that the area surrounding Kandahar was always volatile, and, fighting season or no fighting season, our intel told us there were Taliban in that small farming community in south Helmand Province.

While I was out on the concrete pad checking my gear, Mac began checking my kit and asking me a few key questions about the operation. Marc and I had already checked and double-checked our kit and our weapons, and rehearsed for the mission all we could by quizzing each other on different aspects of our mission plan. I felt as ready as I could be, and you might think that having "big brother Mac" looking over my shoulder would be unwelcome. It wasn't. This is how special operations are done.

It's not the guns and gear or muscles and tattoos that make this work. It's the boring stuff: checking, double-checking, and then checking again. When you're operating at the extreme ragged edge of a human being's performance envelope, anything left to chance *will* kill you. So Mac checking me out wasn't a reflection of his misgivings about my ability; it was a much appreciated third set of eyes making sure I was good to go on my first sniper mission as a team leader.

We were still doing our comms checks when a distant electric version of a voice I had heard in the briefing room scratched into my ear through my Secret Service–like headset.

"Break, break, break," the voice said, letting us know it was urgent we listen.

It was the platoon sergeant. We called him "Two-Seven," or just "Seven," until we were back inside the wire.

"All Second Platoon elements, sound off for comms check."

"Looks like you're ready to go; see you in the morning. Happy hunting, bro," Mac said as he trotted back to his teammates in 1st Platoon.

I thanked Mac and listened intently for my comms check. So far the planning and briefing had gone well, and I didn't want to make a rookie mistake and screw up my first radio transmission to my new platoon. The platoon leadership had all called in, and now it was my turn.

I mashed the button on my MBITR and called our platoon sergeant.

"Seven, Sierra-One. How copy?"

Most of our transmissions are hyper-abbreviated, and there's a reason for that. There are lots of people on the same frequency, and clobbering the net with long-winded sentences is just plain inefficient. What's more, if the enemy is listening in on your frequency, it can tell him way more than we want him to know.

In this case, I was indicating who I was calling (our platoon sergeant, "Seven"), who I was (Sierra-One Charlie. Charlie being the letter identification for my sniper team), and that I wanted to know if he had heard me okay (how copy?).

These mouthfuls of a few letters and numbers were based on a scheme someone much smarter than us dreamed up long ago. And just to make it more complicated, the call signs often changed from operation to operation. They worked, so I didn't dwell on them much.

My platoon leader's response came seconds later. "Sierra, Seven. Lima Charlie." (Lima Charlie means just what you might guess: loud and clear.) That was it. I'd passed another test and avoided being the platoon screw-up. In special operations reputation is everything, and you go to extremes to build your rep day by day.

Someone down the line was having trouble transmitting, so my friend James, our radio operator, rushed over and started troubleshooting his gear. In less than a minute he replaced a malfunctioning antenna and loaded new encryption, and our late caller came through on the net loud and clear. James passed his test, too. Everything was a test in a Ranger unit.

We did a last count of our roughly two dozen personnel and took the short ride to the airfield. It may sound strange that in a well-honed fighting unit we felt the need to count noses like we're third graders going on a field trip. But these were hard-learned lessons, and missions had been compromised because a guy was getting just one more thing for his kit or one more weapon and got left behind.

As we arrived at the airfield, we saw our 160th SOAR brothers waiting for us. The pilots had their birds turning as usual, and listening to the high-pitched whine of the helo's turbines and the flapping of the Chinook's blades beating the air into submission helped me snap into the reality of what we were about to do.

What makes it real for me is not being in-country or the mission briefing or mustering on the concrete for FMC. It's getting on the aircraft. This is the hardest step you take because once you're on that bird you're committed to the mission, and the only way you're coming back is either successful or under a flag.

Our 2nd Platoon's motto was "With it or ON IT." We had taken this from the Spartans. "ON IT" was a reference to the shield the Spartan warrior carried, the fighting device that protected not only him but the man next to him. The shield was heavy and cumbersome, and it was the first thing discarded by retreating soldiers. Spartan women would inscribe these words in Greek on the inside of their

Spartan warrior's shield before a campaign to remind him that he either came back victorious carrying his shield or dead, carried ON his shield by his compatriots.

We walked to the ramps of our two birds, bracing against the hot prop wash that hits you all at once. I always thought how unnatural this was, what we do. It was like walking into the mouth of some great and terrible beast, happily offering yourself up to be devoured. It was the hardest part, but it was my favorite part.

I flashed back to Marc's choice to extend his enlistment, forestall college, and come hunting with me one more time—a foregone decision, I knew, even as I tried to talk him out of it. This is what you had to do to be the guy who goes out into the night to find the evil men who cut off heads and drag bodies through the streets, the ones who steal others' sons and force them to make their so-called jihad and convince others to blow themselves up to indiscriminately kill their own countrymen.

I stepped up on the ramp and made my way to a cargo-net seat hard against the skin of the aircraft. My life—as well as the lives of my fellow Rangers—was in the capable hands of 160th SOAR's Night Stalkers. The rest of the chalk (the number of men would fit into one helo) loaded, I stuffed my earplugs in my ears, smiled, and thought, *I'm on a helicopter full of Army Rangers, my face is covered in camo, and I have a sniper rifle. LIFE IS GOOD.* The cabin lights clicked off, and our blacked-out Chinook lifted up from the Kandahar airfield and banked left.

It was a short flight to the objective area—just enough

time to rehash what I'd heard in the mission brief and bounce that against what I learned during my Ranger training, as well as the hard lessons I'd learned during earlier rotations to Afghanistan. It's easy to go into information overload if you don't check yourself, but for better or worse, I figured I was as prepared for this mission as I could be.

The birds zoomed into the landing area, and the pilots made a combat flare, yanking the nose of the Chinook up to 30 or 40 degrees above the horizon to abruptly stop their forward transit. No matter how many times I've experienced this, I couldn't help tugging on my tether, thinking that if the ramp came open we'd all tumble out the back of the helo. Once all forward motion stopped, the pilots planted the birds on the ground, the ramp opened, and our platoon sergeant signaled for us to stream out of the bird.

Once on the ground, I stopped squinting behind my ballistic glasses and began to orient myself. The prop wash from two Chinooks is like being in your own personal hurricane, so we moved away from the birds as quickly as we could.

I took in the dark landscape and checked my wrist compass. The target was seven klicks from our landing zone. I scanned the horizon for tracer rounds, a sort of early-warning system to see if we were walking into an ambush. It was all quiet, and the lead squad got up from their crouched positions and moved out.

During our mission brief back at KAF just a few hours ago, our movement to the objective areas was a red line drawn on a map, cutting through hedgerows and tilled fields. Now, as we looked through our NVGs (PVS-15 night vision goggles), it was an expanse of green-tinted blackness with pitch and defilade spread before us as far as the eye could see. When we did our mission brief and reviewed the imagery of the objective area, three-story houses were just gray squares. But that meant there could be dozens of windows—and each one could hold menace.

Staff Sergeant Reggie was out front setting a pace that I knew from experience could kill a man, but we matched him with relative ease. Without a word, the platoon silently fell into their order of movement, fanning out to take advantage of the open terrain. We set off at a brisk pace for a reason: we were completely exposed on this open ground, and the faster we moved, the less vulnerable we would be.

Staff Sergeant Reggie's torrid pace paid off, and we arrived at the target compound about 2330, ahead of our schedule. We all moved out to take up our pre-briefed positions around the compound. A shadow governor who used to be a Taliban fighter was now the dictator of this village. While there were many others like him dominating other villages, we had the intel and the opportunity to snatch this guy *now*. There would be many others we'd grab on future missions.

I moved quickly past the target building to where I could see a vantage point that allowed me to cover two intersecting roads, the fastest routes to and from this target area. We were close to the village—maybe 30 meters—and seeing those buildings in three dimensions was jarring.

Marc and I set up shop behind a small wall that gave us just enough cover. I started finding ranges with my range-finder, memorizing distances and landmarks so I wouldn't have to do the math in my head during a firefight. Meanwhile, Marc tuned up his optics.

I continued to finely tune my setup, cradling Miss America and scanning the area around the compound. I knew the assault team was moving on the house, and all hell could break loose at any moment. It struck me how different this village was from the ones I'd encountered in my previous rotations to Afghanistan. It was the quietest, most orderly village I'd ever seen. All the doors and windows were shut, and all the lights were off. All the roads were clean, the hedgerows were straight, animals were inside and secure, and there weren't even any dogs barking.

That told me something important. The Taliban bastard who controlled this village had imposed, and was enforcing, a strict curfew. Everyone who lived there had battened down the hatches because they knew retribution would be coming if they didn't strictly comply with this Taliban-imposed curfew, and nobody was testing it. That meant that anyone who we saw moving about in the village at this time of night was most likely a Taliban fighter. In a lot of ways, this bad actor was making our job easier.

I continued to scan the area I had under sniper observation as the assault team made its move on the compound. A gun team set up about 10 meters to my left. I walked over to see who was leading it. It was Sergeant Lips, a good guy to be teaming with. We discussed having Marc use his optics to help Lips and his gun team direct their fire if we needed to light up the enemy.

I looked through my sniper scope and saw that the assault team had done their work quickly. They had marched everyone in the compound out into the courtyard and were checking them for weapons. I had no idea whether the Taliban leader we'd come to snatch was among that group or not, but I put that curiosity out of my mind for the moment and kept scanning the roads and the buildings for any signs of danger.

Staff Sergeant Bill eased his way into our position and checked on Marc and me, as well as on Lips and his team. I was confident I could handle a lot with just my sniper rifle, but having Lips and his machine-gun team near me gave us an extra edge if it came down to taking out a vehicle trying to make its escape from the compound or wasting a group of Taliban trying to rush our position.

It sometimes feels odd being a Ranger Sniper. You are sitting away—sometimes far away—from the action, and you know your buddies who are kicking down doors are going up against a ruthless enemy. We've lost countless Rangers—as well as other special operators—to booby-trapped houses and enemies lying in wait to ambush them. Still, you have to force your training to kick in and just do your job. As one of my platoon leaders once told me, "You're not their mom."

Things were calm, and we were talking with Staff Sergeant Bill about how peaceful the scene in front of us was. The Afghans that the assault team had gathered up and walked out into the courtyard seemed quiet, even docile. And still, no lights had come on in the village, even after what we assumed was quite a commotion as the assault team took down the Taliban leader's house.

"Taliban doesn't mess around when it comes to their curfew," Bill said. His voice was hushed, just above a whisper.

"They run a tight ship. Not even a dog out in this neighborhood," I whispered back. I forced myself to remember that what seemed serene could still blow up in our faces.

Staff Sergeant Bill started to say something about how clean the village smelled. That was unusual, as most Afghan villages had raw sewage running everywhere. If we couldn't smell the village from 30 meters away, it meant that this was a prosperous little place: they had clean water and were able to at least move their sewage away a bit.

Suddenly, the radios came alive. It was the assault team leader giving us an update on progress inside the compound. We had our man, and now we were going to go next door to his neighbor's house. Our assault team had evidently extracted intel that his next-door neighbor was a bad actor, too.

"Better go," Bill said. "Got to adjust One Gun," he said, referring to the machine-gun team to the north.

"Roger," I replied.

"You guys have this intersection?" Bill asked Marc and me.

Marc gave me a nod, and I replied, "Yes."

"Okay, good," he said. "I'm moving Two Gun down one," he said, meaning he was relocating Lips's machine-gun team to a small intersection east of us, about 100 meters away.

"Roger, Staff Sergeant," I said. "We got this."

As he left, and I could see him adjusting our outer security positions to encompass our now-larger area of operation.

Lips and I agreed that if we were ambushed by an enemy lying in wait in the area surrounding the village, one of us would move to whoever made contact first, and we'd fight our way out of the village together. We were only about 50 meters from the compound and had a good overwatch position.

The radios came alive again. It was the assault team leader. "We've got this joker and his buddy. We're moving out. Prep for exfil in five mikes." That was a welcome call. The mission had gone smoothly. We had our target plus one, and we hadn't taken any casualties.

Marc and I watched the assault team march our two flex-cuffed and hooded captives toward the exfil point. We continued to maintain overwatch while the rest of the Afghans the assault team had assembled in the courtyard ambled back into the compound. We learned later that the assault team had "cleared" all these people, meaning there were no MAMs (military-age males) or anyone else who posed a threat to us.

We walked about five klicks to our exfil point and met up with our 160th SOAR brothers. The flight back to KAF was routine, meaning our pilots didn't have any RPGs shot at them. Once back at KAF, we dropped our kit and mustered for our AAR. Major Dan confirmed that the two guys we had snatched were definitely bad actors. We handed them off to some no-name three-letter-agency guys, most likely CIA. We learned later that they had turned them over to the Afghan police, who would bring them to trial on formal criminal charges.

If this mission sounds antiseptic and "quiet," that's because it was. But it was more typical of Ranger missions than the Chechen sniper mission described in the previous chapter. This is important, because most of what people have been exposed to about special operations has been the kinetics. It's special ops guys rolling in on a target with massive firepower and blowing the enemy to shreds. It's like what a high school buddy asked me when he heard I was going to be a Ranger: "Oh, so you're going to be Rambo."

But the majority of Ranger missions are not about kinetics; they are missions just like this one. We are the ninjas who quietly sneak into your house in the dead of night and snatch you out of your bed, often without waking your family. On this mission, as we learned during the debrief, a Taliban governor who'd been terrorizing an entire village for years surrendered meekly once he saw about 1,500 pounds of Rangers with glowing green eyes hovering above his bed.

This is what direct action is all about and why Rangers are typically the first choice for this kind of mission: we operate in total stealth mode for as long as we can, but if things go to hell in a handbasket we can light up the enemy with overwhelming firepower.

3

SUGAR SHACK

There had been a lull in the action, and we hadn't been called out for a mission in almost a week. That meant training, training, and more training, something that was vitally important but wasn't what we were here in Afghanistan to do. We worked in shifts, sifting through ISR (Intelligence, Surveillance, and Reconnaissance) feeds, and our officers scoured the intel cells for targets. To put it in civilian terms, we were looking for work.

It was still a month before the beginning of fighting season, and our past experience told us this was the time when the Taliban would move their people, foreign fighters, weapons, and drugs into position so they could be prepared to wreak mayhem once the spring thaw came. While we didn't expect there to be any major Taliban offensives this early in the fighting season, we wanted to be outside the wire prosecuting actionable targets.

It was late afternoon, almost dusk, on a cold Afghan day when we got word that we had good intel and a possible mission that night. Runners were dispatched, and we were told that all personnel needed to assemble in their tactical operations center that evening. That was all we were told, and for reasons of operational security there was little speculation. We knew we would learn more in the TOC.

The importance of operational security is drilled into us from day one as a Ranger. When your entire reason for being is to conduct high-risk/high-reward missions, one small security breach can completely compromise the mission and get you and your buddies killed.

Inside the wire at KAF we had not just U.S. military personnel but professionals from other U.S. agencies; soldiers and civilians from every member nation of our coalition forces; U.S. and Afghan contractors providing services from meals to construction; Afghan interpreters who accompanied us on our missions; and others too numerous to name. That's all by way of saying we discussed nothing of an operational nature unless we were in the TOC.

As I walked into the TOC and saw the elements of two platoons—2nd Platoon and a Reconnaissance Platoon, along with headquarters components like K-9s—settling in and getting ready for our intel briefing, I immediately understood that this was going to be an important mission. As I've said, most of our missions were platoon-size ops. Now we were loaded for bear with over two platoons' worth of Rangers.

During our intel briefing we learned that a high-value target—smugglers in a vehicle coming back from Pakistan—would be moving along a major supply route between Pakistan and Afghanistan that night. This MSR was southeast of Kandahar and was familiar to us. Both Pakistan and Afghanistan are somewhat primitive countries—Afghanistan much more so than Pakistan—and they don't have networks of highways like the ones we're accustomed to in the United States. In most cases, there's one way in and one way out, and you could count all the major highways in Afghanistan on the fingers of one hand. Operationally and tactically, that made our job easier.

Afghanistan basically has an agricultural economy, with a big part of that the growing of opium poppies, which are the raw material for heroin. In addition to opium poppies, Afghanistan is also the largest producer of cannabis (mostly as hashish) in the world. There are few facilities in Afghanistan for turning large amounts of that raw material into the finished product, so the opium poppies and cannabis get trucked to Pakistan to be turned into finished drugs.

In return for this raw material for drugs—which is a major source of income for the Taliban and allows them to buy weapons—the Taliban ships money, manufactured goods, and fighters back into Afghanistan. And often, the trucks and cars coming back into Afghanistan also carried the piece parts—shaped charges, blast caps, detonators, and the like—that the Taliban used to make the IEDs (improvised explosive devices) that were so feared by our troops.

Anyone who has followed the news about the conflicts in Iraq and Afghanistan over the past decade and a half knows about IEDs. These weapons have been more deadly to our troops than anything else that the enemy has thrown at us. They're easy for terrorists to build and incredibly difficult for our troops to find and disable. And as we devise ways to defeat one generation of IEDs, the enemy ups its game and builds better ones. Pakistan was shipping sophisticated IED parts that were made there or in places like India and China, and we knew we needed to interdict them. For any soldier fighting in Afghanistan, nothing feels better than stopping the enemy from building IEDs.

Our intel told us that the vehicle we were going to intercept soon after it crossed the border from Pakistan into Afghanistan was carrying weapons, materiel, and money. Most important, these smugglers were going to deliver their cargo to some Taliban leaders who had shipped the raw material for drugs to Pakistan and were now waiting for their payment. That meant our U.S. Drug Enforcement Agency, the DEA, was also involved in this mission.

The crux of this mission was capturing these smugglers so we could interrogate them and have them lead us to the Taliban bosses who were the big fish. We had intel from the DEA, mostly concerning drug smuggling, drug production, and money laundering. The DEA was able to put the pieces together, but they didn't have the manpower to take action against these kinds of targets, and that's where we came in.

Taking out a car full of knuckleheads was easy; a drone strike could do that with the press of a button. We wanted more. We needed a way in the door, to get inside the Taliban's drug network. Capturing these smugglers could give us the leads we needed to start tearing down the Taliban's supply chain in Kandahar and the rest of Helmed Province.

Our plan was straightforward, but it had many moving parts. We were going to intercept this passenger vehicle at a truck stop on the MSR just inside the Afghanistan border. This "truck stop" was nothing like the big, well-lit travel plazas we have in the States. Basically, it was a handful of shacks, a small family home, and a couple of gas pumps. The whole operation looked like it had survived the apocalypse, but just barely.

Because Pakistan and Afghanistan are such primitive countries, gas stops are few and far between. This truck stop, a gas station run by one guy and his family, was the only gas for hundreds of kilometers along this MSR. Whether you were traveling east or west, you had to stop for gas here or you wouldn't be able to finish your journey. So the good news for our plan was that we were going to intercept a stationary vehicle and not try to stop a moving one—something that's hard enough to do in the daytime, and even harder at night.

For this mission I was with the Reconnaissance Platoon, and we would be the backup plan to stop the vehicle if it blew 2nd Platoon's barricade. Marc and I would also provide overwatch for the main assault force, albeit from over half a mile away. Second Platoon would land close to the truck stop at the precise moment our intel told us this car was going to arrive and would set up positions to capture the truck's occupants once they stopped for gas.

I was the sniper team leader, and Marc was my spotter. First Platoon would remain airborne as a QRF (quick reaction force), prepared for any contingency—for example, if the bad guys in the car saw our Rangers coming toward them and instead of heading their warnings to stop, started to flee east or west along the MSR.

Since this mission would involve a total of six Chinooks—at least two of which would possibly remain airborne for an extended period—we were going to use a FARP our Army engineers had constructed close to the Pakistan border. These FARP sites are important pieces of the operational puzzle because, as our 160th SOAR buddies like to say, "When you're out of gas, you're out of business."

While the Chinooks are good aircraft, they're notorious fuel hogs. Load them up with a few Ranger platoons and all their heavy weapons and those birds suck down fuel like a drowning man sucks down oxygen if he makes it to the surface of the water. While some FARP sites—especially the ones our Marine Corps comrades build—are large and complicated, this one was pretty basic. It was literally just concertina wire surrounding some fuel blivets (big rubber bladders) in the middle of a huge patch of desert.

It might seem that two full platoons of Rangers as-signed to take down one vehicle full of smugglers is over-kill, but it goes back to our mantra, "Hope for the best, but plan for the worst." As I've said, this was the time of the year when the Taliban moved their people, foreign fighters, weapons, and all the rest into and around Afghanistan. The vehicle we were after could be stopping for gas when a truckload of Taliban and foreign fighters were also at the truck stop. Those were the kinds of situations we needed to be ready for.

After the briefing, we assembled outside the TOC and checked our gear and our comms as we usually did. Our reconnaissance platoon had to hustle, as the plan was to have us launch first, land covertly about 10 klicks from the truck stop, and then move quickly to get to the objective area and set up overwatch positions for the main assault. We did our muster and a last check of our kit and weapons, and caught our ride to the airfield to board our 160th SOAR Chinooks.

It was a short ride—about a half hour—to our objec-tive area. After we landed and streamed out of the Chi-nooks, our platoon leader formed us up and we started moving north at a brisk pace. Even in the green glow of our PVS-13 night vision goggles, we were reminded of how desolate most of Afghanistan is. We were at an elevation of several thousand feet, and the moonscape we walked across was devoid of life—no animals or vegetation of any kind.

We were about 2 klicks into a brisk but unhurried trek

toward our objective area when our radios came alive. We got updated intel from KAF that the target vehicle was going to get to the truck stop ahead of schedule, and we needed to advance our timeline and get to our overwatch position *now*.

Things had been pretty methodical up to now, but all of a sudden they got frenetic. Our platoon sergeant led us on a virtual dead run for the 7 or 8 klicks we had to cover to get to our overwatch position. Meanwhile, 2nd Platoon, the assault element, was still at the FARP site. They had to gas and go in a hurry to get to the truck stop in time.

We got to our overwatch position and set up quickly. The MSRs snaking through Afghanistan are pretty basic, but this one was *really* basic. It was the type of road made by hand with stone and dirt and centuries of consistent use. It followed the contour of an ancient mountain range that was reduced to hard rock monoliths, maybe 400 to 500 feet tall.

As we settled into position along the ridgeline, I checked my wrist compass and followed its bearing to the horizon. Sure enough, there were headlights. As I said, Marc was spotting for me for this mission, and he put his LRF (laser ranger finder) to work.

We started to build a mental "range card," which is a basic military drawing of the area around us.

"Distance to target area?" I asked Marc.

"I have seven-eight-zero to the nearest trucks," he said. Marc didn't bother saying "meters." In our abbreviated way of communicating, just giving the number of meters was our default mode of communicating distance. My eyes followed his, and I slued my IR (infrared) laser to where I thought he meant.

"Yep, that's the one," he confirmed.

"What distance do we have to the truck stop itself?" I asked.

Marc worked the problem for a moment. "Eight hundred to the part I can see. It's eight-fifty to this hut-looking thing. What's that even for?"

Marc was a cheerful guy, and you wouldn't guess we were doing anything more than checking out a deer stand before hunting season. As was true in almost every mission we went on in Afghanistan, there was some random structure with no discernible purpose. Try as we might to fully understand the Afghan culture, their ways were not our ways.

"Okay," I said. "We'll call that tangle of trucks the parking lot. See anything near this goat pen?" I asked. I pointed again with my laser, circling an area I wanted his eyes on.

"Goats?" Marc responded with a chuckle, as he found my laser spot. "Hmm . . . just goats, seven-nine-five. Call it eight hundred meters, Balls."

That seemed good enough for me. We ranged a section of road between us and the truck stop and quickly memorized that distance as well.

I was carrying my bolt-action Mk-13 mod 2, our "big gun." It fired the .30 caliber cartridge. Because I knew I might have to stop a vehicle quickly, this large cartridge was just the ticket. I also knew that any shots I had could be a half-mile. To give you an idea of what kind of stopping power this shell has, the .30 caliber is the go-to round for hunters going after moose, elk, and bighorn sheep. I knew I had the right weapon to stop a passenger vehicle.

Our overwatch position was about 800 meters from the near side of the truck stop, and while we were well concealed, we had a pretty much unobstructed view of the action. The rest of the Recce Platoon was watching our backs to ensure we weren't ambushed from behind or overrun by Taliban coming out of nowhere. It was "Hope for the best, but plan for the worst" on steroids. But having said that, the reason we were in Afghanistan was to decimate the Taliban. It would be a *good* thing if they attacked our position. We just needed to be ready and ensure it wasn't a fair fight.

A few meters away, Marc was backing me up with his .30 caliber during close-in fighting as far as putting out rounds in a hurry. This is by way of saying that if the truck stop turned out to be full of Taliban or foreign fighters and it hit the fan, the enemy would have to think twice before trying to rush our position.

I flashed back to our intel brief and instantly identified the vehicle we were told to intercept. It was a Toyota pickup, probably the most common kind of vehicle used in Afghanistan, and it was entering the truck stop from the east. It had four passengers in it. At the same time, we could see 2nd Platoon rushing to get into position to encircle the truck, make it stop, and grab its passengers.

Just like that, our plan was falling apart. The target vehicle was moving slowly, and 2nd Platoon was using its 250-lumen tactical lights to signal the car to stop, but it didn't. It didn't stop at the truck stop at all but just kept moving. Time for Plan B, and we were it! Our Recce Platoon sergeant was on the net with Major Dan trying to get clearance for me to shoot the truck, ideally through the engine compartment, and stop it.

It now seemed like a near-death experience, when time slows to a crawl. *Where's the damn authorization to shoot?* I thought. I watched the truck through my scope, and I could see that its headlights would soon fade behind the large rock outcropping between me and their route through the truck stop. If I waited until I could see them again, 2nd Platoon would be in my line of fire, and shooting at the truck would present too great a risk of me creating a friendly casualty. I considered—then rejected—the idea of just taking the shot without permission and dealing with the consequences later.

All this was going through my head while I was building and rebuilding my shot and adjusting my math. Marc was looking through his optics and feeding me the minute corrections he saw as the truck continued to travel. And every second I'm thinking, *We're gonna lose this sucker.*

As I'm hoping, *praying*, for the authorization to shoot, I'm breathing in cycle, timing each inhale and exhale, ensuring that I'm ready to fire at a split-second's notice when the call comes. Seconds stretched into minutes as I waited for the call. As the truck's lights began to fade from view like a setting sun, I began to give up hope. *It's too late* . . .

"Shit, lost him," Marc said under his breath. He was mirroring my own thoughts.

Suddenly, my earpiece came alive. It was Major Dan. "Sierra is cleared to engage vehicle," he said.

My right ear was bare, and I had my right cheek pressed against the stock of my rifle. I was inhaling and exhaling evenly, slow and steady, trying not to disturb my crosshairs focused on the target.

I was looking at a wall of granite, a grainy black and green monolith in my night vision scope. I knew the car was there, and I knew how fast it was going. I've practiced this shot more times than I can count, but on a stationary target, and one that was only about 400 meters away. We had started tracking this vehicle at 1,000 meters, and now it was rolling, unseen, toward my cross hairs at 840 meters. *Inhale, exhale, inhale, exhale* . . .

I was trying to get the lineup just perfect and put my cross hairs on a spot on the road behind the mountain. I knew the truck would be the same distance away as the gas station, and I knew from studying the map where the road was behind the mountain, so I pictured exactly where that should be, measured in my scope, and placed my crosshairs on that spot. Marc and I had already calculated vehicle speed, and I could see the point in my mind. If we had calculated correctly, my bullet would meet the target vehicle at 840 meters.

I was dialing in my scope elevation when I heard my platoon sergeant key his mic. I knew what he was going to say—that we no longer had eyes on. I squeezed the trigger before he could utter the words I didn't want to hear as my own thoughts came to the fore: *We didn't load up two full platoons of Rangers to do nothing.*

The recoil of my .30 caliber sent the big rifle back into my shoulder hard, while the scope accelerated toward my eye. But I never lost my sight picture, and I saw my cross-hairs fixed on where I *knew* the target was all the way through the violent recoil. By the time my rifle settled, 190 grains of copper-jacketed lead should have dipped below the false horizon between us and the target. Never losing my sight picture was an indication I had gotten off a good shot.

I was confident the round had gone where I wanted it to—into the engine block of the target vehicle.

The net cleared and I simply said, "Sierra, shot, out." There was an eerie silence for what seemed like an eternity before I heard a calm voice say, "He's slowing down."

Then another voice: "Roger, looks like he's stopping . . . break . . . we have four pax exiting the vehicle." (Pax means persons.) "Now the hood's up." Marc and I formed a mental picture of the vehicle's passengers staring into the engine compartment of the stopped vehicle, trying to figure out why their car had stopped.

Another voice broke in on the net. "Must have engine trouble."

Marc cast me an incredulous look that I could barely see in the dark, but I could read his thoughts: *You did it!*

I could hardly believe it. Sure, we train for it, we're confident, and we *do* think we're pretty damn good. But we also calculate first-round-hit probability. Over half a mile, in the blind, on a moving vehicle, and that .30 caliber bullet had to go straight through the aluminum engine block of that smuggler's vehicle and make the engine seize.

I had a Toyota truck back home, and a picture of my truck's engine compartment flashed into my head. I pictured the places the round would need to strike to stop the target vehicle so quickly. Did it hit a harmonic balancer? Did it bore straight through the aluminum engine block? It must have buried in the motor somehow, because a miss or a near-miss would have sent frag into the cab, or else made enough light and noise that the drivers would know they were being shot at.

If I had been off a little and hit the oil or cooling system, an oil or coolant leak would eventually disable the smuggler's vehicle, but its occupants might still be able to drive all the way to Kandahar in the cool night. If I had been farther off and hit a tire, it wouldn't go flat for a mile, and with their momentum they could roll even farther than that. There weren't any other options, so the only conclusion we could draw was that the engine must have seized.

In all humility, I began to thank my lucky stars, but my platoon sergeant quickly shook me back into reality.

"Sierra, did you just shoot a truck you couldn't see and

stop it with one round?" he asked. Saying he sounded incredulous would be a gross understatement.

"Yep!" Marc chimed in, quicker than I could think of what to say. "That's why we call him Balls."

Marc was right. There were no lucky stars to thank; we were trained to exacting standards by the best instructors in the world at both the U.S. Army Sniper School and the Special Forces Sniper Course. We were in the business of the impossible, and we were *expected* to be able to make shots like this.

We maintained our overwatch position while 2nd Platoon secured the truck stop and the area around it. Soon the radios came alive with abbreviated Ranger commands.

"Mike Alpha Two-Three, move up and lock them down," the Alpha Company Platoon Sergeant barked, referring to 2nd Platoon's third squad leader.

The commands continued. "Mike Alpha Two-Four, move your guns north and south and lock down that MSR," referring to the weapons squad leader, who was in charge of all of the company's crew-served and anti-tank weapons.

"Two-Two, push out security." The assault platoon was already moving to form a large semicircle around the objective area, and now they were being told to expand it. "Send some guys to One and start helping them clear those big rigs!" One was the first squad. We never knew what a big rig would contain—anything from Taliban or foreign fighters to weapons destined for the wrong hands.

We'd practiced this kind of maneuver many times before, so there was no need for the squad leaders even to click an acknowledgment.

Seconds after these commands were uttered, I watched as 1st Squad and 2nd Squad moved to surround all the vehicles at the truck stop while the machine gun teams moved to the periphery of the truck stop to cover the other squads.

Perched at our observation point, we looked through our NODs as Mike Alpha Two-Three moved his squad up to the stopped smuggler's vehicle. Within seconds, they had the car's passengers covered with their infrared lasers.

We watched—and also picked up the radio chatter— as the third squad leader and his Afghan interpreter began to question one of the smugglers—the one, I was to learn later, who was in charge. The Ranger standing next to the squad leader turned his red overt (meaning visible) laser on this smuggler while the squad leader and his interpreter shouted commands at him.

Finally, after enduring a barrage of questions, the man being grilled told his interrogators that their car had just stopped!

I turned to Marc, and even in the dark I could see his toothy grin as he gave me a light punch on my left shoulder.

"Must be a piece of junk, just like your truck back home."

Marc convulsed in silent laughter, and I managed to muffle a chuckle.

I always caught hell for my old Toyota truck, and here it was again.

At the truck stop, 2nd Platoon was now searching the big rigs, the gas shacks, and the family home. All they found were a few tons of sugar, candies, and snack cakes (Pakistan's version of Little Debbie cakes). The assault force wrapped up their questioning—and unwrapped quite a few snack cakes, too. We quickly came to the conclusion that the only way to label this mission—now and forevermore—was "Sugar Shack."

We got the word to get ready for exfil. We were perched in our rocky overwatch position, and I knew there was no way to get down to the truck stop below and link up with 2nd Platoon. I'd be lying if I didn't tell you I was disappointed. We were eager to see the results of our handiwork. I wanted to know if I could take home that totaled engine compartment of the vehicle I'd stopped dead in its tracks and mount it as a trophy, but I knew better than to ask.

The 2nd Platoon leader called for exfil, Marc and I broke down our position, and we began to walk west, straight out into the flat plane, which reflected moonlight like a dusty mirror.

Second platoon broke down their position, collected their smugglers, and also moved west, into their own desert, separated from ours by the dark, looming rocks that used to be great mountains.

When we were 5 or 6 kilometers from the MSR, we took a knee and listened. Soon we heard the unmistakable sounds of the incoming Chinooks. The reassuring sound of 160th's Night Stalkers grew louder and louder, and soon there was a noise of dust, roaring turbine engines, and the glowing static rings of the rotors. This glowing effect is caused by dust and static, and has been named the Kopp-Etchells effect for Ranger Benjamin Kopp, who was killed in action near Marjeh in southern Afghanistan in 2009, and Corporal Joseph Etchells, a British solider also killed in 2009 in Afghanistan.

We loaded up our four smugglers and took them back to KAF for further interrogation so we could learn the location of the Taliban leaders they were supposed to link up with. Time was of the essence because we knew that when they didn't show up for the scheduled rendezvous, the Taliban kingpins would be suspicious.

Back at KAF, we handed these guys off to an Afghan team and a western advisor for what we figured would be a long interrogation. Like many missions we conducted in Afghanistan, we did our part and then we were done. It was frustrating not having the big picture, and something you never got used to.

For a Ranger Platoon, if there's one thing that we constantly remind ourselves of, it's that there's no "I" in team. I'd just made the most technically difficult shot in my Ranger sniper career, but all I could think of was how we all had accomplished our mission and were returning to KAF without any Rangers killed or wounded.

When we got back to the TOC for our debrief, and our seniors began to piece together what had happened during our mission, I got kudos from Major Dan, our recce platoon sergeant, and some other platoon leadership. They knew they could count on me in a pinch, even if it meant putting my ass on the line.

This mission had a positive result; it just took a bit longer than we had expected. Even under intense interrogation, the four smugglers we captured didn't know—or wouldn't divulge—where the Taliban leaders they were delivering this materiel to were located. But our intel analysts had watched the feed from one of our UAVs (on-station unmanned aerial vehicle) and noticed that these smugglers had stopped in the disputed tribal areas near the Pakistan-Afghanistan border and conducted a linkup with another vehicle.

Our overhead assets followed this vehicle as it moved into Afghanistan, and the next night, 1st Platoon followed that vehicle all the way to the Taliban leaders' compound and captured him. He turned out to be a high-value target. He was brought back to KAF, interrogated, and then handed over to Afghan authorities.

Without putting too fine a point on it, this was like many Ranger missions, where persistence pays and it's a total team effort to complete what we came to do. I was happy—but I still wanted that trophy of the totaled engine compartment.

4

WORKING WITH THE DEA

Our entire platoon was buzzing. The previous evening, another Ranger platoon had gone on a night raid into Kandahar. During the mission, someone tried to bushwhack one of our snipers. Equipped with night-vision gear, he had seen the Afghan man become alerted to the Ranger's presence and fetch his AK-47. The Afghan noticed our sniper on the roof and took aim. As soon as he did, the Ranger sniper, well ahead of him, broke a perfect headshot, followed by four or five more shots to the head for good measure.

I don't think our sniper missed any of those shots, and it was a gruesome job putting this guy's face back together to try to identify who our enemy was. It turned out that the man who was taking a potshot at our Ranger sniper was the bodyguard of a Haqqani family member, and he also happened to be a cousin of then-Afghan president Hamid

Karzai. This was unsurprising and points to one of the many gray areas in Afghanistan: it was often difficult to sort out your friends from your enemies. Without getting into a political argument, let's just say our partnership with the Afghanistan government was an uneasy one.

It's worth pointing out that our Ranger sniper providing overwatch on a pretty routine mission getting shot at by some random guy is completely normal. We expected that kind of thing to happen on every mission. Kandahar is like every other city and village in Afghanistan—everyone is armed. It was a challenge to "win the hearts and minds" of the Afghans when the only way to survive was to treat every civilian as a potential enemy. And that didn't just mean military-age males. It could be an 80-year-old man with a cane who was wearing a suicide vest, or a woman with a weapon hidden under her burka, or even a child with a weapon. We learned the hard way that most of these people didn't want us here, and they were willing to take extreme measures to kill us in any way they could.

What *was* clear from the encounter I just described was that the Afghan fighting season was underway. Spring was coming, and like the weather, things were only going to get hotter. You might think that would make us worried or afraid or wish that our rotation would soon be over. In fact, we knew we would be in Afghanistan well into the fighting season, and it was exactly what we wanted.

Those of us who had done a few turns in Afghanistan knew that "operations tempo" and felt time went hand in hand. Winter deployments were a grind, and you eked out your time hitting any and every possible target. During the fighting season, the sheer volume of Taliban and foreign fighters meant we would conduct missions nightly, sometimes two or three a night.

We showed up at the TOC for our briefing when we usually did, around 1700. Since we own the night, and we wanted the odds stacked in our favor, that meant nighttime ops were our bread and butter. We'd often come back from a mission in the wee hours of the morning, debrief, shower, get some chow, and then sleep until early or mid-afternoon the next day. Luckily, the time difference between Afghanistan and home base at Fort Benning was almost 9 hours, so it was more like a 3- or 4-hour difference in your schedule, like moving from Los Angeles to New York. You got used to it eventually, but it took a while.

During our intelligence briefing, we learned that we had targets on the outskirts of Kandahar city. "Outskirts" was good news, because it meant we'd be forcing action against the enemy but didn't have to navigate the treacherous tangle of the city itself, where every window, door, or alley was a potential ambush. Kandahar is a huge city—maybe half a million people live there—and it's been around since the days of Alexander the Great. That means the buildings are jammed together every which way. It's not an orderly city, like we're used to in the United States.

All this is by way of saying that if you were on a night mission in Kandahar proper, you had to guess at everything. Was a pile of rubble the remains of a decayed adobe building or a hiding place for a jug containing a homemade bomb? Were those goods left out overnight in a bazaar because they had little chance of being stolen, or were they too dangerous to move because they were filled with explosives?

In the suburbs or the countryside, dangers were a little easier to discern, but there was always something confounding going on. I never understood why every home had an old hubcap full of nuts somewhere in its living space, or why a basket placed over some chickens was often placed on the ground next to a swaddled infant. It always struck me that stepping on a wicker basket with chickens underneath in the middle of the night would be alarming, to say the least. You never got used to it, which means you were on high alert 24/7. Just when you grew accustomed to swaddled-looking things being infants, they turn out to be homemade explosives. Most of the time that wicker basket was over some chickens, but it could also be hiding a land mine.

When our Ranger platoon or company showed up at the TOC for a briefing, we often met people from other organizations who had some role in the overall U.S. effort there. You've probably heard the terms "joint" and "interagency," but it's worth explaining them here, because you'll hear them many times during the rest of my story.

"Joint" simply means one or more of the U.S. military services working together. We've learned though many conflicts that we're more successful taking on an enemy in a conventional war when all the services—Army, Navy, Marine Corps, and Air Force—work in unison. For a long time we couldn't figure out how to work together, so the Army worked in one area, the Marine Corps in another, and so on. The events of 9/11 were the catalyst to change that, and now all the services train together in exercises and then work and fight together in major conflicts like Operation Enduring Freedom.

We've also learned the hard way that leaving things solely to the military leaves our domestic agencies in the dark, which undermines the entire point of the Global War on Terrorism, which is to prevent terror attacks on U.S. soil. That's where "interagency" comes in.

For example, there are *seventeen* U.S. intelligence agencies alone. Some, like the CIA and NSA, are familiar to most Americans because they're in the news. And then there are a whole host of other groups, like the DEA, CBP (Customs and Border Protection), and ICE (Immigration and Customs Enforcement).

Many of these agencies were working in Afghanistan because this is not a conventional war. In a conventional war, an enemy takes territory that isn't theirs and we go in force-on-force and throw them out. An example of this is Desert Storm, where Saddam Hussein invaded Kuwait and our coalition drove him out. Most of today's wars are far more complicated. And if there is a poster child for this different kind of war, it's Afghanistan.

Our and our coalition partners' mission in Afghanistan wasn't just to kill Taliban. It was also helping the government establish itself in areas the Taliban controlled. Another mission was stopping the flow of drugs from Afghanistan to the West. Yet another was to help the Afghan people do things we in the West take for granted, from having schools for both boys *and* girls to having at least semi-reliable cell phone service, to bringing more modern farming and construction methods to remote towns and villages.

All this is by way of saying that when you showed up in the TOC for a briefing, you never knew who you would meet or, more important, whose needs would be driving your mission that night. If some other agency was there, it might be their needs.

So it was often left to us Rangers to analyze the intelligence (typically from multiple sources) and determine what the "go/no-go" criteria were before conducting the mission. That was ideal, but sometimes it wasn't that way, and other agencies worked with us to meet our combined needs.

I can't tell you how many times we showed up at the TOC, saw some guy in civilian clothes—typically a nondescript guy in a polo shirt sporting a beard—who only told us his first name and almost never told us what organization he was with. Major Dan and the rest of the command team would know those details, but that information was Top Secret and Compartmentalized, meaning that only a few of us were read into the full details of the mission.

All that most of us Rangers knew was that we were to go to this place and do this or that or the other thing. And sometimes we'd just be told, "This is Bill (or John or whoever), and he's coming with us." Sometimes this interagency guy would "pitch" us as to why what we were being asked to do was important. We'd plan and brief the mission like we always did, except our "new guy" was now hanging out with us.

I'd be lying if I didn't admit that this was a bit unsettling, and it was something I never got used to. We were trained as Rangers, which is all about "one team, one fight." But when the people you're supposed to be working with to accomplish a dangerous mission go out of their way to make the point that they'll tell you only what they think you need to know—well, let's just say that it made me feel a bit like a hired gun.

For this mission, our new friend was a DEA agent. He was part of the briefing that evening, and he made his pitch. When I say pitch, I mean just that. In Afghanistan, all of these three-letter agencies were there to assist us, not to direct us to do anything. So, just as on many previous such missions, our DEA agent painted the picture as convincingly as possible and in such a way that our leadership—and all of us, for that matter—could see that the risk-reward equation worked out in such a way that we'd go on the mission.

As I've said, Afghanistan is a major producer of the raw material—opium poppies and cannabis—for what eventually become street drugs. We were told that our target was a guy who lived in a compound where there were tons of opium poppies ready to be smuggled into Pakistan to be turned into heroin. We were told that this target was a major producer, and just like back in the States, that meant he must have important connections.

Just as they do in the United States, our DEA agent assured us that the street value of the drugs could be in the millions, maybe tens of millions. That seemed to be the norm for all of the missions like this that we were asked to take on. It was as if the agent felt he could work us into a frenzy by convincing us that the cache of drugs was so vast that we were on the most important anti-drug strike ever.

I was still digesting this briefing as we sat in our 160th SOAR Chinooks and curved up and away from KAF. Personally, I was dubious about the overlap of the war on drugs and the war on terror in general. I wondered how much of what we'd been told was fact and how much was fiction. We had excellent reconnaissance of the area, with good imagery from a variety of overhead assets, and I could see from the images just how our target was living. His little house had dirt walls, and he had dung cooking fires. He looked for all the world like a simple Afghan farmer, but our DEA agent had told us he was a major drug dealer. But what did I expect, that this Afghan farmer would have a mansion and a zoo like Pablo Escabar?

We were briefed that the guy we were going after had two compounds. He lived in one compound with his large family—maybe a dozen people overall. The second compound was separated from the first one by a road and was unoccupied. This was likely a workshop used to process drugs. My platoon, 2nd, was assigned to take down the compound where the dealer and his family lived, while Mac and 1st Platoon were assigned to secure the other compound.

We landed well away from the objective area and moved toward the compound at our usual breakneck pace. But as we got to the outskirts of the village we had to change our tactics to honor the threat of IEDs. On this mission we needed to be extremely wary of them.

The IED threat was extreme in Helmand province, and the Taliban encouraged poppy farmers to put IEDs pretty much everywhere around their growing operation. The war in Iraq was over, or damn near, and the bomb makers and fighters who had been operating there found their way to Afghanistan. Our enemy was skillful at using this influx of talent, and now the country was saturated with IEDs.

The poppy farmers were businessmen who wanted to stay in business. For them, sowing the area around their property with IEDs was no more extreme than a store-keeper in a rough neighborhood in America using a pull-down grating to protect his store. The farmers started by putting IEDs in obvious places, like roadways, doorways, and footpaths. As a rule of thumb, if it was easy, it was booby-trapped. And based on what we'd heard in our intel brief, if this guy was as big a grower as we were told he was, we figured he'd damn sure want to protect his operation.

The easy route to his compound had danger written all over it, so we went the hard way. Instead of taking a direct path toward it and going through gates, we walked through crop fields and scaled walls. Poppy fields were especially treacherous, since the Taliban had discovered that our strategy was to target the source of their revenue. All this meant that we had to treat poppy fields as all-but-certain locations for IEDs and other bombs.

As we approached our target, I walked near the front of our platoon, just behind the point man, Sergeant Ryan, the team leader for 3rd Squad. On our left was Jim, our dog handler. His Belgian Malinois was a small brindle similar to a German Shepherd, and it was trained to do two things: smell bombs and attack (and sometimes eat) terrorists. Behind us was our EOD (Explosive Ordinance Disposal) staff sergeant.

Back in KAF I had been picking his brain about how he searched for bombs during a foot movement. His description sounded like something I had learned in sniper school called target detection. It was a tactic useful for finding hidden enemy snipers, and it worked just as well for finding IEDs, trip wires, and other booby traps.

We agreed that I could use my sniper skills to help him look for these dangerous devices. I could probably do this just as well as he could, but he was the only guy on the ground who could render an IED safe or destroy it. He and I ran our plan by our platoon sergeant, and he liked it. From then on, if I wasn't needed somewhere else in our order of march, I made sure I was out in front with the lead element.

Just as important, our EOD staff sergeant was the guy who could accurately identify HME (homemade explosives). Simply walking into an HME lab unawares could ignite a massive explosion. All it took was the impact of a single footfall, or the gust of air from opening a door, to blow the explosive crystals against each other and create enough friction to trigger a massive explosion.

We arrived at the compound without incident, but pretty beat up from climbing and crawling to avoid IEDs. Since Marc and I were the only snipers on this mission, I put him on one end of the outer cordon around the target compound and set up shop on the opposite end. I had my favorite sniper rifle, Miss America, and Marc had his preferred weapon, his SR-25.

In much the same way as the rest of a Ranger task force, Ranger snipers are trained to be flexible. We work together or alone, or augment another weapons system. With our training and optical equipment, snipers have the best "eyes" on the battlefield, and a good portion of our job is to confirm or deny anything suspicious that any other Ranger sees. We can see farther than anyone else, which means that snipers can positively identify a weapon at a greater distance. This is important because seeing an enemy with a weapon defined our "shoot/no-shoot" criteria. I knew our entire platoon was counting on us to identify an enemy before he could take a shot at any of us.

Marc and I were acutely aware of what had happened to our sister Ranger platoon when a terrorist with an AK-47 almost nailed one of their snipers. I could feel my heart pounding as I looked through my night scope at the fuzzy green glow and searched for anything that looked threatening. If someone on the outer cordon around the target area was suspicious of a distant figure or vehicle, he would call for one of us to look at it through our sniper scope and make an assessment. Using snipers in that way afforded us more time and space to deal with a threat—something called "standoff," which meant the safe space between you and a threat.

There are many factors that go into making a successful shot at an extended range—the target, the distance, the wind, the weather, and the elevation, among other things. As part of my Ranger Sniper training, I studied with an aeronautical engineer for several weeks. If you think about it, hitting a target with a bullet is a bit like hitting a point in space with a rocket, so there were strong parallels to my craft. The math we did was part trigonometry, part geometry, and part rapid calculation.

One of the things that attracted me to become a Ranger sniper was that our craft is part science and part art. For example, one part of the job is ranging the distance to a target. We had top-of-the-line laser rangefinders—at least as good as any other military service—but we also practiced range estimation by eye because that's the fastest way to get bullets on a target. It took practice, but we were well calibrated from drilling this and other sniper skills daily.

It always amazed me that the human body could be so well calibrated, often gauging great distances to within 5 or 10 meters, good enough for a first-round hit with a sniper rifle. Knowing range accurately was also important for machine gunners, who could send a swarm of bullets in a concentric pattern 1,500 meters away instead of just one at a time like me with my sniper rifle. That's why, whether it's us or the enemy, snipers and machine gunners working together make for a deadly combination.

Machine gunners and snipers share a number of skills. For example, we both make range cards. You can give this card to the next Ranger who relieves you on overwatch, and he can use it as a reference for windage and elevation corrections. So while many people think of a sniper as a lone wolf working alone, the synergy we bring to the table by working with a machine gun team can be deadly to an enemy.

We knew our assault team was about to move on the compound, and our job as snipers was to have their backs. And I mean that literally, as we'd learned the hard way on missions where we'd lost Rangers. The enemy had a knack for luring us into a trap where we'd move on a house and focus all our attention on what was inside while the enemy snuck up behind us.

I felt we had a good plan to cover our Ranger buddies' backs on this mission. I left Marc to "hunt the gap" with the rest of our outer-cordon security. They were blocking all the main avenues of approach to the compound, and Marc would roam between them to make sure we weren't missing anything. If he found a gap in our security, he would fill it in or call it up. In that case, Staff Sergeant Bill, our WSL (Weapon Squad Leader, pronounced "weasel"), would decide if he needed to move personnel to better cover the assault team.

The assault team conducted a surreptitious entry of

the compound: one Ranger slipped over the wall on a ladder and opened the gate from the inside, while the second Ranger up the ladder stayed on the wall and provided cover and overwatch on the entire compound. Once we all were inside the compound walls, things got noisy. Our interpreter, Zeke, used a bullhorn to call the man out of his house. Within minutes, a clearly confused and dazed man staggered into the courtyard.

The rest of the assault force secured the perimeter, and we continued to have their backs. Within minutes, First Sergeant Hutch and Zeke were talking with the suspected drug dealer. The questioning went okay at first, but then they hit a snag. Hutch had a knack for discerning if someone was lying, and he could follow a narrative with precision. If you tried to make something up or there was an inconsistency in your story, he would catch it. But Hutch couldn't find any inconsistency in this guy's story. He seemed to be telling the truth when he said he didn't know anything about the Taliban, or even heroin, for that matter. What he did know about was cannabis, to the extent that he had grown enough of it to have 5 tons of the stuff sitting under tarps, ready to be made into hashish. We didn't know what that pulpy green stuff was other than some form of cannabis, so we just called it hashish or hash or sheesh, for "sheesha," the local word for it.

While our intel was good, it wasn't perfect, and we noticed another compound close by. We sent a team over to the neighbor's house, but he was as clueless as Smokey (our nickname for the hashish farmer) about the Taliban and heroin. Two houses and just one guy's stash of sheesh. We had expected heroin and a Taliban connection. Could our DEA agent have been this far off?

Major Dan called KAF for clarification. The orders we got back were simple and straightforward: burn the drugs. It seemed uncomplicated enough; the stuff was made to be smoked, so it should be easy to burn it. Rangers were good at destroying anything and everything, and we were especially keen to try out our incendiary grenades on something different. In the end, we tried just about everything short of high explosives (not that we had low explosives) to destroy the stuff, and none of it seemed to work. I think it would take a dozen tires and a hundred gallons of diesel fuel to burn up that much wet plant matter.

By morning, when most of us were manning the walls of the compound, the stuff was still there in smoldering piles of what had to be the world's most expensive compost. I felt bad for the farmer. We had zip-cuffed him, and he had to watch as we burned his stuff.

The morning dawned, which meant we no longer had the advantage of owning the night and were closer to being on an equal footing with the enemy—not a good thing. We packed up our NODs, made sleep rosters, and powered down some MREs ("meals ready to eat," though we called them "meals rejected by everyone"). We were talking with higher headquarters about reconnaissance and other air support, as well as about exfil plans if things got really hot, as they had when we had to deal with the Chechen sniper and his pals in the Musa Qala District.

We had sent Smokey and his family packing, telling them to send the Taliban to his house if they wanted to kill Americans. I felt for the guy. One minute you have 5 tons of sheesha, spring is around the corner, and you're going to finally make some money on last year's crops. The next minute someone has burned up all your stuff and kicked you out of your own house so they could have a war in it. They say war is hell, and it is—it can kill, maim, or wound you, and keep you in constant terror. But it can also snatch away your dreams when a day ago you thought you had a goldmine no one could ever touch.

The sun melted the frost a few hours after dawn, and the people in the villages around us started to wake up and move about. The compounds closest to us stayed quiet, and aside from the Afghans inside them doing necessary things like feeding and watering animals in the interior of their courtyards, the village seemed to stay buttoned up. They knew we were there, and we figured they saw no value in attracting our attention.

So why were we still there? After all, we'd destroyed the drugs we found, and our DEA agent was certainly pleased. But that brings us back to why we were in Afghanistan in the first place. Think of it this way. The DEA's mission was to burn drugs. Our mission was to fight—and capture or kill—Taliban.

When we carried out the DEA's mission, we were essentially burning the Taliban's money. We knew this would tick them off and make them crazy for revenge. That's why we didn't exfil that night but instead did a ROD, so the

Taliban could come and try to kill the Americans who were burning the goods they used to fund terror. None of us Rangers really cared about the drug war, which was secondary to our goal of fighting Taliban.

We continued to scan the villages around us, but no one was coming or going. A few hours before dawn we had sent a team out to place barricades on the main supply route that ran through our area. We knew that if Taliban from the surrounding area were going to mass to attack us, the MSR was the dagger that pointed directly to our position.

Suddenly, two men who looked to be in their early twenties appeared riding one of the small motorcycles that were popular in the region. I could see that they had no weapons, and they just sped down the road and stopped at our barricade. Wary of their hand gestures, Mac and I fired two suppressed warning shots in their direction. They were in a perfect position to call in a mortar or rocket strike against us. Our quiet shots didn't exactly have the desired effect.

Our captain's voice came over the radio: "Sierra-One, this is Six. What are you firing at, over?"

"Six, Sierra, warning shots. We have two MAMs on a moto stopped at our northern barricade," I keyed back.

He pressed his transmit button twice—what we call "breaking squelch"—sending two slow, deliberate "squelching" sounds scratching softly into my ear. I could hear Platoon Sergeant Pack in the background but couldn't make out his words. Then our Caption came back on the net.

"Hey, Sierra, we don't think they realize they're being shot at because of your suppressor, over."

Our 3rd Squad leader, Staff Sergeant Bob, had heard our transmission and decided to take matters into his own hands, firing two rounds from his unsuppressed M4 that tore through the still air and impacted near the front tire of the moto. The driver ripped the throttle, and the passenger on the back barely held on as he whipped away.

"Warning shot, over," Staff Sergeant Bob's voice boomed over the net. I could picture him with a big smile on his face.

"Ho! That dude almost fell off! We almost got a new terp, Sarn't!" Bob's SAW gunner said excitedly. ("Terp" is short for "interpreter.")

"That's why you don't ride two-up on your moto with another dude!" Bob said sagely before cracking another big smile and laughing with his SAW gunner.

Mac and I chuckled along with them from our position a little farther down the wall.

They got the picture, and I thought that our captain was probably right and that suppressed warning shots aren't so good.

The two men had turned left as they sped off. Then we saw them meet up with two more motos. Mac and I immediately scrutinized them with our rifle scopes, trying to guess their intentions. Soon a gang of twelve motos had formed. Now things were getting interesting, and not in a good way.

"Sierra-One, Seven, you have any SA on those motos?"

It was Platoon Sergeant Pack. He wanted to know if we saw the moto riders carrying any weapons.

"Seven, negative. They're four hundred meters out. No weapons, over," I keyed back.

"Roger, keep an eye on them," Pack ordered.

After their little meeting, the motos dispersed in every direction but ours. A short while later they returned, now each of them two-up, which meant they were getting closer to matching our manpower.

Now we were getting twitchy. But then the motos disappeared as suddenly as they had appeared.

The day wore on, and a little after noon Marc came to relieve me. I stayed up on the wall and overwatched our area of operations with him for a while before finally giving in and finding a place to sack out. I was so tired I don't remember if I even bothered to eat.

I'm not sure what woke me, but I put on my kit and helmet and went back to work, probably around 1500. I found Marc, who was shooting the shit with a machine gunner on the west side of the compound. They were pulling security, but all that took was your eyes unless something happened.

We could see the shapes of men on motos riding back and forth in a wood line about 300 meters away. (A wood line is a row of trees at the edge of a field.) Every once in a while they would gesture at us. They seemed interested, but their hurried movements and the terrain obscured their numbers, as well as what they were doing. We didn't see anyone digging; that was good. Digging would mean

IEDs on whatever route they anticipated us taking out of there. I left Marc and the machine gunner and went to find Mac to see what he thought about the action.

I found Mac on a ladder on the west side of the compound, peering through his small binoculars. "Got anything, Mac?" I asked, looking up at him.

Before he answered, he climbed down a rung or two so he wasn't silhouetted over the wall, not taking his eyes off the horizon until he was covered.

"A bunch of guys on motos fucking around in the wood line, all around us, actually," Mac said from his perch. He was frustrated, and we were both a little puzzled. Those were not good guys out there, and they sure weren't the neighborhood watch.

More and more of these motos formed around the periphery of the compound. We were surrounded, but to get to us the enemy would either have to drive through tilled and furrowed fields or come down the MSR single-file.

The Taliban are fierce—and sometimes fanatical— fighters, but they're not stupid. We had our machine guns trained on both of these avenues of approach, and we could have cut them to pieces if they had tried to attack us.

There was an empty fighting hole in the wall near Mac, and I joined him in searching for a shot, looking for anything that would give these guys away. They were our enemy, but, like us, they had been blooded in combat, and they knew what rules we were bound by. They had their own intel that they'd gleaned from somewhere—from KAF or a corrupt councilman or who knows where. The point is, they knew *exactly* what our engagement criteria were. It was pretty binary: ten years of fighting makes you dead or savvy . . . I don't care who you pray to.

It was a small consolation, but the enemy seemed as frustrated as we were. They couldn't figure out a way to get to us. It was a standoff, but it was an away game for us, and soon we would have to walk out of this compound and into whatever they might have waiting for us.

Then, before the sun met the horizon, as we were breaking down our positions and getting ready to exfil, the shadowy motorcycle gang that had surrounded us started to evaporate, and we could see them turning away from us and hear the high-pitched whine of their speeding bikes.

Finally the sun set, and we prepped to move out. We waited until it was fully dark and then headed south to our new exfil point. We made that change when we noticed that they couldn't completely encircle us in that direction, since the terrain to our south was impassable for a moto, which also meant it was unlikely there were IEDs planted along that route. It was tough going, but hard walking is always better than getting your legs blown off and never walking again.

We waited at our exfil point for only a short time before we heard the reassuring sound of the Night Stalkers' Chinooks beating their way toward us. There wasn't any chatter as we each sat alone with our thoughts. Mine were focused on wondering how our intel for this mission had gotten it so wrong.

Back at KAF we dragged into the ready room where

we staged our fighting kit and weapons. Twenty-four hours of continuous operations doesn't count the planning process. We dropped our kit and made our way to our briefing room and our AAR. It was a pretty standard debrief. We talked about the ways to make holes in the tough Afghan adobe, what extra supplies we needed for the next mission, and other ways we could up our game.

The thing we talked about the most was the farmer and his sheesh. We had spent a whole day and most of a night trying to destroy his stuff. We messed it up really good, in the sense that now the farmer couldn't sell it. But I guessed we only actually destroyed at most one of the five tons. A thermite grenade had barely made a dent in this stash. I could see a few other Rangers shift uncomfortably in their seats, just as did I when we started discussing the best way to destroy hashish.

Maybe this operation was a bust, and the DEA's tip about smugglers didn't pan out. We had spent 24 hours outside the wire and had zero follow-on intel from the night's operation. Our agent seemed pleased during the debriefing, but I noticed First Sergeant Hutch give him a sideways look when he said we had done good work.

The next afternoon, Mac and I got up early and went to the "European" chow hall. KAF had four chow halls, one for each coalition partner, and we were both adventurous eaters.

We were as close as any brothers and still are to this day. But our backgrounds were vastly different. Mac's father was in the military, and he had grown up mostly on the East Coast. His upbringing and his values as an adult were conservative, to say the least. I had grown up out West, in Colorado. My upbringing had been much more liberal, and my values reflected that.

"Hey, Mac," I began as I watched him shovel in what could almost pass as gourmet food. "You ever do a mission like this before, where you go after a guy for growing drugs?" I asked the question to broach the subject, because I remembered that back in the summer of 2009, Mac and I had patrolled through cultivated fields of 8-foot-tall cannabis plants as far as the eye could see.

"Shit, no!" he exclaimed around a mouthful of food. He swallowed quickly and added, "Remember '09? That's practically the national crop around here. We would have to march abreast with the whole battalion armed with flamethrowers from here to the Hindu Kush to destroy all that stuff!"

I chuckled a bit in response; he had hit that nail on the head. In the summer of 2009 we did almost an entire 7-klick movement through fields of cannabis.

"I mean, they don't even have *booze*; they aren't allowed to drink," Mac continued. "What are we really going to do about it?"

"Right!" I agreed enthusiastically. There were millions, probably tens of millions, of hectares of cannabis being cultivated here, and its use was ubiquitous among the Afghans.

I was reassured that my trusted friend felt the same

way I did, and our conversation lulled as we continued eating. I tried to process exactly how I was feeling. I was conflicted. On the one hand, I would proudly fight anyone, anywhere, for my country, death and injury be damned. On the other, I imagined how I would feel if I had to spend the rest of my life in a wheelchair if my legs got blown off by an IED while we were burning cannabis for the DEA. Worse still, how could I reconcile the loss if one of my brothers died doing that?

"Did you know that back home, pot is nothing more than a petty offense?" I asked Mac.

"I've read about that. Boulder, right?" Mac acknowledged. "How does that work, man?"

"Denver too, bro. It's the same as a jaywalking ticket," I explained.

"Hmm!" Mac affirmed, nodding to me while he chewed the last of his meal.

I continued, "Man, I'm not getting my legs blown off for this—"

Mac, sensing my rising emotion, interrupted me. "I got you, bro; we probably just went after the wrong guy. The poppy is paying the Taliban. That's what they expected us to find."

I nodded my agreement.

"Let's get back to the TOC," Mac said. "Maybe they have a different target line for us." We were both hoping that we were changing our strategic direction.

We policed up our trays and empty drinks, and headed back to the TOC. I felt like Mac and I were on the same page regarding the futility of trying to burn up all the sheesh in Afghanistan. I wondered how the rest of my Ranger buddies felt about it.

When we got to the TOC, the rest of the guys were still filtering in. Our DEA agent was talking with Major Dan and First Sergeant Hutch. Sergeant Reggie had gotten there early, which was his usual practice, and he'd already heard the gist of what we were expecting for this night's operation. Mac and I drank some coffee and chatted with our team leader while we waited for the official word.

Sergeant Reggie explained that "someone," "somewhere" from within the enormous but amorphous U.S. intelligence community had pinpointed the location of a major player in the drug trade. Reggie started passing around maps and aerial photos of our proposed objective area.

I immediately focused on the photography. They were in "black hot" thermal. This means that they were taken with special cameras that capture images by measuring heat. The hotter something was, the darker it would be. In this case, I could see the black spot at the center of our target compound, with four or five larger, nearly black spots around it.

I knew from experience that represented the residents of the compound and a cooking fire. I looked at the macro picture, a zoomed-out version of the same image, and started committing to memory the temporary names and numbers we had assigned to the roads. We named the roads after sports teams and numbered the buildings in sequence. This was our normal tactic and was nothing more than an aid to memorization. It was disposable information, and after a couple deployments it was easy to commit what we needed to know to memory and then immediately "brain dump" when the mission debrief and AAR were complete.

When the TOC was filled up, Staff Sergeant Bill took charge and called for everyone to take their seats while our senior leadership chatted among themselves. The briefing was pretty standard. We had done a similar mission the night before and we were going to do it again.

After the briefing, we gathered on the concrete pad outside of TOC as we always did, checking comms and doing PCIs (pre-combat inspections) on our gear. Normally I would feel nervous and excited, but also superhuman before a mission. Just the sight of kitted-up Rangers, my brothers and peers, gave me supreme confidence, not to mention pride. Here I was, surrounded by the baddest men on the planet, any one of whom could have been my childhood hero. They were the guys I watched John Wayne, Robert Mitchum, and Lee Marvin portray in the movies I grew up loving. These were the men who bumped back against the monsters of this world. They were noble, selfless, and wickedly determined to visit the ruthless violence of Ranger justice upon our enemies.

We call sniper work "overwatch." I said it in every briefing when I explained what I was doing on our mission. I always began by saying, "Rangers lead the way, gentlemen. My call sign is Sierra-One, and my task and purpose tonight is to provide overwatch and precision fires."

It was, and still is, the thing I am most proud of: the exhilarating duty to watch over these bloody-handed heroes. It was a dizzying responsibility and still overwhelming for me to think of at times. But this night I felt blank; the normal balance of fear and pride was mute because the mission was different. I know now that this was a survival instinct: my internal system was shutting off unnecessary components to maintain focus on the task at hand.

On most missions you knew it was worth getting your legs blown off because you were stopping the guys who made and emplaced IED's, trafficked in people and weapons, brutalized women, and killed indiscriminately. But this operation took a bigger leap of faith than that.

In Afghanistan, food crops aren't worth the water it takes to grow them because Pakistan dominated the Afghan market with much cheaper imported food. There was almost no way to make cash from your crops unless you grew hemp or cannabis. So many of the farmers grew crops just for subsistence and grew cannabis for the money they needed to make a living.

I was scared, to be sure: that was a given anytime you're in country. No one *isn't* afraid of being maimed or killed or of losing their brothers. This mission was happening, and I had better do it right, just like I had better do it right every night. If I made a mistake it was unlikely that *I* would pay the price; it would cost someone else instead. *That* was unacceptable to me. Even though I found this mission distasteful, and one that went against my personal morals and ethics, I had a higher moral imperative to keep faith with my leadership and to make sure I overwatched the platoon and had their backs.

I looked around at the men in 1st and 2nd Platoons and thought that every day we were closer to the boiling point that would officially kick off the fighting season. We were going back to the outskirts of Kandahar, maybe 10 klicks from where we had been the night before. I hoped tonight we wouldn't be the casualties that precipitated this year's fighting. We had already drawn first blood on the enemy in the city, and if I knew one thing, it was that they knew SOF (Special Operations Forces) had a vested interest in shaping the area to set the conditions in our favor when the fighting season did begin.

This time, we were going against our SOP (Standard Operating Procedure), and we weren't being quiet about it. Our cunning enemy wasn't going to come out and fight us any longer. They could just wait and work behind the scenes until the American and ISAF troops withdrew. (ISAF was the International Security Assistance Force—the NATO-led security mission in Afghanistan.) We had to make ourselves an irresistible and easy target. At least we would have the full complement of Task Force Merrill taking the fight to them.

We loaded up on our Chinooks, and my apprehension melted away. Our platoon motto, "With it or ON IT," was our mantra, and it gave me a goal to focus on. There was no home, no politics, no quitting, no second-guessing— just inertia. We were now as unstoppable as gravity. The birds taxied to the runway, and the engines throttled all the way up. Their tremendous power made the airframe shudder, and soon we were airborne and momentarily weightless.

Once airborne, I pulled out a small map I had made of the target area and a red pinch light (the kind you put on a key chain) and studied the route we would take once we were on the ground, noting the prominent intersections and the building where we thought we would find our heroin grower.

Our flight to the objective area in our Chinooks was pretty standard—if you can call roaring over the Afghan countryside at 175 knots—almost 200 miles per hour—in the middle of the night in blacked-out birds standard. It was a quick flight, probably less than 30 minutes, and each of us was alone with our thoughts and our mental preparation for the mission ahead.

By the time we landed, I was fully in the zone. It felt like a low boil of anger mixed with glee, but tamped down by the iron discipline the Ranger Regiment instilled in us.

The birds pitched as they dropped below the treetops, landing with a lurch in a rough field not yet readied for the coming growing season's crops. I followed the rest of my chalk off the Chinook's back ramp, racked a round into the chamber of my M110, and started walking so fast my shins burned before we hit the wood line and picked up our infiltration route to the objective area.

When we got to within 50 meters of the compound, we established our standard security cordon around the target area while the assault force headed for the compound.

The assault team conducted a surreptitious breach of the compound, defeating a chain and padlock and slipping through a vehicle gate. Once the assault team had the main house under their guns, Zeke activated his bullhorn and began his scripted instructions.

"Inside the house. American forces have you surrounded. Come out with your hands in the air."

It was a simple script, but who the heck knows what he was adding to the loud torrent of the five languages he spoke. It must have been compelling, because soon the man of the house, along with what seemed like a dozen children and half as many wives, staggered out. You could see they had dressed hastily.

Zeke was generally shy and reserved—he was barely old enough to buy beer in the United States—but he had been on countless missions and took charge of his role with confidence. He commanded the women and children to go to one end of the walled-in courtyard and the men to go to the other. It only took an instant to verify the ages of the younger males, a twelve-year-old and a fourteen-year-old, both of whom we deemed non-threats. The father would be the one we were interested in, and his sons were sent to the women-and-children side of the courtyard.

When we were planning the mission, Marc and I agreed we couldn't both be on the ground and cover everything we needed to, so we split up. He had my favorite job, proactively roaming our immediate area by hunting in the gaps in our outer cordon. I was going to do my work from a second-story rooftop in our target compound. We could cover everything, and if we stayed on top of it, we could support each other. It wasn't easy spotting for your sniper partner from a distance, but we knew from our training that it could be done.

We were on opposite ends of our cordon, and I called Marc to let him know I was moving. "Sierra-Three, Sierra."

"Go for Sierra-Three," Marc called back.

"Roger, I'm climbing." This was my way of telling Marc that I was leaving my position on the ground at the cordon to go inside the compound. Once there, I planned on using a ladder or stairs to get to the rooftop. I continued: "When you get down here, you'll see that Two-Gun has moved off the MSR. You'll see them hidden under the cypress trees. I've got visibility to 1,200 meters, but your shots should be inside of 500 meters."

I gave him a few more landmarks and distances, so he had a rough sketch of the area: an intersection at 200 meters, a house at 350 meters whose occupants seemed to be awake, a heap of dirt that could be a fighting position at 100 meters. If he had to flex in that direction in a hurry, these details could get him into the fight faster.

"Copy all," Marc replied.

I made my way to the breach. Tonight we were dealing with a big compound with an accommodating roof. It would afford me the longest views and bit of room to move and take cover if they bombarded us with RPGs. I paused at the gate and in a low voice called out, "Friendly, coming in." We wore noise-canceling amplified earphones that made whatever I said sound like a shout.

The young Ranger on the other side of the wall answered my password with "Come on in."

He may have been a teenage private on his first rotation to Afghanistan, but he was still 300 pounds of bulletproof plates and hard Kevlar knuckle gloves, and he had a grenade launcher, a tomahawk, and a machine gun. (Our M4A2 rifles have full auto instead of burst—another perk of being in the Ranger Regiment.) I knew that all he did was work out and drill to exhaustion day in, day out. It was a steep learning curve to go from recruit to Ranger, and for most people the first 18 months in the Ranger Regiment are a grueling blur of pain and trial. I gave him a nod as I walked in.

When I entered one of the compound buildings, I did a double take. There were six large tarps covering what had to be five massive piles of what appeared to be at least a million dollars' worth of heroin.

Maybe we're on to something, I thought. *Maybe the intel was right this time and we're taking down a major drug supplier and cutting off the Taliban's cash source.* I shook my head and started climbing up to my vantage point. The flat terrain meant I could see 360 degrees and make out the glow of Kandahar City proper on the horizon. I keyed my radio and called Marc. "Sierra-Three, I'm up, send a laze," I said, asking him to help me see where he was by sending a laser point from his rifle.

I didn't bother identifying myself; Marc would know who I was from what I was saying to him.

A Green Infrared laser beam shot out from the west

from Marc's weapon-mounted laser, and I traced it back to his position.

"Sierra-One, you got me?" Marc asked.

I shone my own laser over his, swiping up and down, as if nodding with a 1,000-meter-long beam of green light. It was all the confirmation he needed, and we blinked our lasers off almost simultaneously.

Moments later, I heard a commotion below me. I climbed down from my perch and joined the assault squad. They were gathered around the piles I'd passed earlier. But it turned out the tarps weren't covering heroin poppies: they were covering hashish. This guy was just like the farmer on the mission the day before, growing the stuff to make a living, not to supply the Taliban.

I could hear First Sergeant Hutch becoming animated. He wasn't happy about what was going down. Major Dan and our RTO (Radio Telephone Operators) were working their radios, trying to get to the bottom of what was happening. It was clear to me they were angry that we were sent on another mission where the DEA had lousy intel.

I tried to stay out of it. My job was to look out, not in, but it took discipline to stare out into the quiet, empty night instead of focusing on the bustle and noise inside the compound walls. As I remembered our previous mission, I admit that I wasn't looking forward to spending another day with the desert sun beating down on me in the hopes the Taliban would roll in on us.

I wasn't going to have a hand in burning this farmer's cash crop, but I also wasn't looking forward to spending another day next to a smoldering pile of plant matter, either. And I certainly wasn't looking forward to dragging my ragged nerves and exhausted body through what was certain to be an IED-littered landscape the following night to get to our exfil spot.

If I knew anything, it was that the Taliban would wise up to us and ambush us on the way out, or that we would hit an IED.

It didn't take long for our orders to come down from headquarters. Just like our last mission, KAF ordered us to burn the hashish. Despite last night's trial-and-error efforts, we still had no idea how to do that quickly or effectively, but we started in anyway. The assault force scavenged some gasoline from one of the farmer's sheds and went to work on the massive pile of drugs.

By now I was getting frustrated, and I assumed we would be fighting a pile of mulch instead of Taliban. This wasn't what I'd signed up for, and it wasn't what Rangers came to Afghanistan to do.

Suddenly, 2nd Platoon's Sergeant Pack came across the net.

"Break, break, break; all copy." He didn't have to use his call sign: by this time we all knew our platoon sergeant's voice.

"We will exfil in 5 mikes," he began. "Assault," he continued, referring to everyone inside the compound, "start breaking down your positions."

"Break"—he paused to follow radio protocol. "Outer cordon, you'll lead us to the HLZ with Stryker, break."

I joined the Rangers to get my gun into the fight, but I have to admit I wasn't disappointed we were pulling out of there. Two nights, two busted missions where what we were told would be there wasn't, so we punted and ruined some guy's life. I just wanted this bogus mission to be over.

I pulled out my tiny map to confirm we would move west.

"Two-four," Pack ordered. "We'll pick up you and your gun to the west. Everyone else collapse on Phase Line Broncos, over."

I put away my map and climbed off the roof of the house. Then I headed to Phase Line Broncos, the north-south running road that ran along the western side of the target compound. From there we cut west through fields and irrigation canals until we came to a flat open spot the Night Stalkers had preplanned.

As I sat on the hard canvas seat of the 160th SOAR Chinook during our exfil, I couldn't forget that sinewy and leathered farmer. His darkly tanned skin showed a long life of brutally cold winters, blistering summers, and harsh desert sun. But it was his eyes—set deep in his almond-shaped face—I'll never forget, showing first bewilderment, then resignation, and ultimately hatred.

He didn't look like a bad man, and he seemed a bit old to be a fighter. Nothing we knew, nor anything we learned about him that night, connected him in any way with the Taliban or of being responsible for any violence against co-alition members. And I didn't come to this conclusion alone. I'd overheard some of the conversation between First

Sergeant Hutch and the DEA agent we escorted to the target. Hutch wasn't happy with what the DEA had us do, and he explained why in purple words. It confirmed my worst suspicions, and I realized why what we were ordered to do sucked so bad.

We had been ordered to burn all 20 tons of the cannabis pulp that the farmer and his family had processed throughout the winter. They had watched somberly as all the capital they were depending on for the coming season's supplies and equipment went up in smoke. We had accomplished our "mission" that night (as other Rangers had done on other nights working with the DEA), but what had we really accomplished?

It wasn't hard to reach the conclusion—hell, it was a near certainty—that by burning his crops we probably killed that man, and maybe his family, too. With their entire cash crop gone, they would need some other means of income. For a farmer with no crops to sell or money to put in a new crop, the options were few and grim.

We knew from experience that Taliban stooges would likely hire him to house, hide, and feed their fighters. If he was unlucky, his children would be treated like property by these men on their way to wage jihad. His sons might be pressed into the fight rather than learning to work the land and provide for their families.

If he was lucky—and in this case that's a relative term—his home would become a way point on a smuggler's route as they moved bits of IEDs, weapons, medical supplies, and other things they needed to take the fight to us. If he was *really* lucky, he would just be expected to be a source of intel for the Taliban, monitoring the MSR for any sign of our coalition forces.

But as much as we wanted to believe those "lucky" scenarios, our collective experience of over a decade of dealing with the Afghanistan Taliban told us it was wishful thinking to hold out any hope for this farmer. The more likely scenario was that he would be found by a Marine Corps or Army sniper's bullet while he tried to dig a hole for an IED the Taliban ordered him to plant.

Another scenario, equally bad, was that in exchange for his family's safety, he would be forced to wear a suicide vest and make his way into the nearest coalition base and wreak havoc on our forces.

Then it would go downhill from there. His sons, bound by honor and religion to avenge their father, would have nowhere else to turn but the Taliban or Haqqani. It's difficult for Americans to understand, but the Afghani and Muslim customs of honor are incredibly strong. They are bound by religious teachings, as well as tribal ones, to avenge a family member's death. But they aren't focused on the Taliban when they do this. They're focused on us. We were the ones who came out of the night and destroyed their livelihood, which forced their patriarch to turn to the Taliban just to make enough money to survive.

As I mulled this over, it didn't take me long to come to the conclusion that all we were accomplishing on these missions were creating terrorists. That's what made what we were doing so recklessly shortsighted. Worse, we were

risking our lives to create these terrorists and perpetuat-
ing the cycle of violence we had come to Afghanistan to
end. While I got going after poppies to cut off the Taliban's money supply, rolling in on simple sheesh farmers
and destroying their livelihood and effectively sentencing
them and their families to death made no sense at all.

What we *were* pretty certain of was that doing this to
a simple farmer who was making his living in the same
way farmers in Afghanistan had made their living for centuries wasn't helping us accomplish a mission that made
any sense for our country or for our coalition partners.
Turning hard-up farmers into Taliban or Haqqani stooges
wasn't going to result in fewer Taliban or Haqqani: it was
going to make *more* of them. And from a risk-reward standpoint, trying to get to a well-protected compound where
this farmer was doing the sensible thing and protecting his
only livelihood certainly wasn't worth our legs getting
blown off when our strike force found the inevitable IED.

As soon as we got back to KAF we dropped our kit in
our ready room and headed to the TOC for our AAR. Normally an AAR was informal, our time to air grievances
and speak frankly about what had happened on that mission. Rank was rank, but if you had a criticism, this is
where you had a chance to say it. It was part of our constant effort to fine-tune our strategy, improve our tactics,
and adapt to our enemy.

Tonight was different, and the bitterness of some of
our team members bordered on contempt. We all were still
in a state of disbelief that we had been ordered to do what

we just did. We may not have had degrees in criminal justice, and none of us were well versed in the sea of American foreign policy directives that were suddenly intersecting in our Tactical Operations Center, but something wasn't right. Saying "If it walks like a duck, and quacks like a duck, it's probably a duck" comes to mind as I reflect on this mission even today.

We were in the TOC the next evening and it was too quiet—I'd never seen it that quiet. A room full of high-testosterone alpha males always has a sort of buzz about it, but there was none of that tonight. We got our intelligence dump, and all the day's developments were relayed to us. We were shifting our focus to direct action against some Taliban and Haqqani targets. After a quick brief about who these guys were, and our trigger criteria (events significant enough to cause us to launch) were for this mission, First Sergeant Hutch let us all know why things were so quiet. Hutch began by saying what I had been thinking.

"Men, we won't be working with the DEA anymore. I don't personally give a shit if every Afghan wants to smoke sheesh until their eyes glow red. If the DEA wants to go after these guys, they can go out and get them on their own. I didn't come here to burn marijuana, and nobody in my company is getting their legs blown off for that."

Hearing a leader we trusted—one who had been carrying out orders far longer than we had—say this was one of the high points of my six rotations to Afghanistan. He said what needed to be said, and he said it with conviction.

First Sergeant Hutch then said that Major Dan and the rest of our leadership agreed with his assessment, and that they had taken those concerns to the top of the 75th Ranger Regiment. Hutch reiterated what some of us already knew, which was that *all* of Afghanistan smokes sheesha. It's as ubiquitous as alcohol in the United States. If you really wanted to wreck the Afghanistan economy and turn every last person against the United States, then you just had to burn all their cannabis crops.

But we also knew that, unlike sheesha, the Taliban and Haqqani had their hands in almost all poppy production. That much more lucrative market was indeed funding terror, and until we got our arms around that, the Taliban would be well funded and well armed, and we wouldn't succeed in our mission.

5

SAVING THE CAVALRY

We had operated out of Kandahar for several months now and were pretty settled—meaning we knew the area, knew the enemy, and had learned enough through trial and error that we felt, to use a sports analogy, that we were in midseason form. We knew that the enemy we were facing in southeastern Afghanistan was dangerous and ruthless, but we were beginning to get the upper hand. And now that it was spring and fighting season was in full swing, we knew the enemy would come at us, and we'd be able to take out more of them.

That didn't mean we were taking a victory lap—far from it—but we felt we would be able to go on missions to kill more Taliban while losing fewer Rangers. That was based on the experience we'd gained, and especially what we'd learned about the tactics, techniques, and procedures the enemy used in this area. I'd felt this way before on previous rotations to Afghanistan, and it usually meant just one thing—we were going to get tasked to move to a completely new area and start all over again.

It was a normal day at KAF. We were training, doing PT (physical training), and cleaning our weapons when our platoon sergeant came to us with a WARNO (warning order). This was the usual way we got the word about what might happen next. It was an informal kind of communication that was used all the time, and all we were told was that we would be moving—and soon. Some of the usual hotspots were mentioned: JBAD, Khost Province, Ghazni Province, and a few others. Obviously we wanted to know more, but our platoon sergeant just left it at "somewhere up north."

That wasn't very satisfying, to say the least, but we knew the drill. We all began to pack up, taking our full fighting kit and weapons and trying to decide what to leave behind. Some of that was our personal stuff, but some was gear that could be air-dropped to us in a contingency. And then we waited.

We didn't have to wait long. The next night, we got the official word: We were moving from KAF to Mazar-i-Sharif, in Northern Afghanistan. That meant only one thing: there would be a fight there, and getting into a fight is exactly what Miss America and I, as well as my fellow Rangers, came to Afghanistan to do. I could feel the adrenaline rush already. I'd heard stories about how hot the fighting got around MES (Mazar-i-Sharif), and I was ready.

Now things rocked on fast-forward. As night fell at KAF, we did our final MWE (accounting of men, weapons and equipment) and prepped for our flight to MES. It wouldn't be helos for this trip; MES was almost 900 klicks from KAF. The only way to get us there was in the venerable C-130 Hercules, the four-engine military transport that has been around since the 1950s.

As we loaded aboard our two C-130s, we were all anticipation. We hadn't gotten any additional intel on what we'd be doing once we got to MES, or why we had to get there in such a hurry. Back when we were all civilians, we would have had a thousand questions and would have demanded answers. But that wasn't the military way, it wasn't the Army way, and it sure as hell wasn't the Ranger way.

The Hercules flight was uneventful—meaning no one shot at us—and we landed at Mazar-i-Sharif International Airport just before dawn. We taxied to the military side of the airport and caught a ride to Camp Marmal, the German-built base that housed the troops of many nations that were part of ISAF. There were about 5,000 ISAF troops from over a dozen nations in Camp Marmal, so we figured we wouldn't have any trouble blending in.

We dropped our gear in a small tent camp that the base commander had cordoned off for us. It was secluded from the rest of the base—something that was always important to us. That was the good part. The not-so-good part was that Camp Marmal was *really* basic. While KAF wasn't Club Med, it was upscale compared with this. Here we had four tents: one for our leadership, two for our assault force, and one for our TOC. We were living on top of each other, at least twenty people to a tent. And since we didn't have a ready room like we had at KAF, that meant that we lived with all our gear strewn all over the place.

Still, we settled in as best we could, accounted for all our men, weapons, and equipment, started absorbing some of the intelligence from the area, and tried to get back on a normal sleep cycle. And just like you'd do if you moved to a new town, we scouted the base out to find out the best options for everything from food to places for PT to where you could barter for some swag from the troops of one of the other ISAF nations at Camp Marmal. There was even a local bazaar, which was just a tractor-trailer full of cheap junk. Think of it as an Afghan Stop & Shop, with things like cheap cigarettes, knock-off toiletries, and gas station snacks like chips and other junk food.

At first, we didn't have any big missions, and I began to wonder what the rush had been to get us here. Some missions took us northeast to Kunduz Province, while others took us to Maymana, the capital of Faryab Province, near the Turkmenistan border.

A typical mission would put us on Chinooks flying to Kunduz. Once there, we'd refuel and then launch to the surrounding area to do a mission—typically going out in platoon-size units to snatch a Taliban leader and bring him back to Camp Marmal for interrogation. Another mission would put us on C-130s to Maymana, where we'd remain in that Dutch-controlled forward operating base, sleeping through the day and launching missions at night. We basically did three types of missions there: night raids against high-value targets, clearance in a zone of large areas where intel couldn't pinpoint a specific target, or investigating NAIs.

The pace was grueling, and we didn't have our full complement of 160th SOAR Chinooks to carry us every night. That meant that the Night Stalkers were augmented with some National Guard Chinooks. The National Guard birds were older airframes with older weapons, mostly M240 machine guns, instead of the miniguns on the SOAR birds.

The National Guard pilots were as ballsy as anybody I had ever flown with, and their dated guns were meticulously maintained by their aircrews. What they lacked in sexy, cutting-edge technology they more than made up for with their professionalism. The Army worked its Chinooks and their crews hard. While it might say "National Guard" on the side of their birds, they were as good and as busy as their regular Army counterparts.

I had been farmed out before, meaning we were so far from the primary targeting lines that the 160th SOAR couldn't justify the risk of carrying us. They had logistical considerations as well and would often fly for more than one Ranger strike force. Everyone was maxed out, and the Night Stalkers were no exception.

We call them targeting lines because they're straight lines connecting one bad actor to the next. We'd get intel on one Taliban leader and capture and interrogate him, and that would often lead us to another one, who'd lead us to yet another. That was a best-case scenario, and if we could have our pick of missions, these were the ones that were most effective in terms of effort spent and results achieved.

We quickly realized that many ops out of MES would have weak, or nonexistent, targeting lines. Up here in Northern Afghanistan, we didn't always have actionable intel. It was like the ghosts we hunted in Musa Qala all over again. These Taliban fighters—and, more important, their leadership—were well connected, well resourced, and as easy to spook as an old buck deer during hunting season. They traveled light, left little trace of themselves, and could vanish into the Hindu Kush, whose 20,000-foot peaks have been the Afghan people's fortress for thousands of years.

Once obscured in this western portion of the Himalayas, Taliban could travel anywhere they wanted, from Iran to Pakistan to Turkmenistan to Tajikistan and even to India if they were determined and had the right connections. You only need to glance at a map to see how enormous this area is and how easy it is for an enemy to melt away and elude us.

Worse, the alternating expanses of desert and mountains these areas contained accounted for some of the most severe and impassable terrain on the planet, and our enemy used this desolation to their advantage. Worse still, border checkpoints were perfunctory at best, if there was any "border" at all.

Given all this, there was very little ISAF presence in

these far-flung areas. I never understood why we were conducting missions in these remote areas in northern Afghanistan when the Taliban were killing hundreds of their countrymen in cities in southern Afghanistan every month. To me, it seemed a bit like filling sandbags in your living room to try to keep your house from flooding. But as I said before, these missions were thought up by people way above my pay grade. Like Rangers before us, our role was to execute policy, not create it.

The battle rhythm I describe above was a constant grind and was wearing us down. We went on lots of missions without a whole lot to show for it. Sure, we went on those missions to Kunduz, Maymana, and elsewhere and scooped up lots of Taliban, but after a while it began to feel like we were playing Whac-A-Mole. There was no endgame in sight, and we sometimes felt like Sisyphus trying to roll his enormous boulder up the hill, only to be doomed to watch it roll down again.

Mac and I were in the TOC looking over the day's intel when we got a hint that an entirely different kind of mission was coming together. Our officers, who were always hunting for a mission where we could take the fight to the Taliban, caught wind of an emerging crisis. And as opposed to the missions we'd been conducting night after night, this one involved saving our own guys.

We learned that somewhere out in the vast expanse of desert to the east of us, a Forward Operating Base full of Army Cavalry Scouts was cut off and surrounded by fighters from the IMU (Islamic Movement of Uzbekistan).

The Cavalry Scouts at this FOB were there to conduct VSO (Village Stability Operations) for that area. This was something the Army and Marine Corps had been tasked with in many of our wars—keep the enemy out of the villages and let the people who live there have as normal a life as possible and gain confidence that the government could protect them. The idea was to eliminate the leverage that the Taliban—or in this case the IMU—had on the locals. This would create a favorable environment for our Special Operations Rangers to take out the Taliban who sought to keep the local civilians under their thumb.

The intel we got told us the Cavalry Scouts had been doing this for a while: providing a security presence for the local villagers, helping them with building projects, holding juras (a sort of Afghan town hall) with village elders, and basically establishing trust with them. It was the "hearts and minds" aspect of what our military, and especially the Army, had done for the longest time in many of the conflicts we've been involved in over the years.

The Cavalry Scouts at this FOB were in a tough place to begin with and out on a limb with respect to support. Let me put it this way. The Chinook is the fastest helicopter in the U.S. Army inventory, and this FOB was over an hour away by Chinook from the closest coalition support. They'd been doing okay during the winter, but as the spring thaw came and the enemy became more mobile, the IMU fighters began to mass in the area around the Cavalry Scouts' FOB. To say that our Army brothers were a juicy target doesn't begin to describe how vulnerable they were.

The intel kept coming, and it kept getting worse. The IMU fighters in the area had surface-to-air missiles and plenty of RPGs that could easily take down any of our helicopters, so the 150 or so Cavalry Scouts at this FOB were running low on everything: food, water, ammunition, you name it. These men were heavy hitters, one of the Army's premier units, but now the powers that be had put them in such a tenuous position that an enemy using Cold War–vintage weapons had cut them off and virtually surrounded them. They were in deep trouble, and it was getting deeper by the hour.

The Cavalry Scouts had a dirigible floating above their FOB that was put there to provide reconnaissance for the area surrounding them. We had a satellite feed from their dirigible, and we used that to augment our intel and try to determine how many enemy we would be up against. Even with the best intelligence, we had no way of telling exactly how many IMU fighters were in the vicinity, but our educated guess put the number in the thousands.

The puzzle started to become clear. Not only were the Cavalry Scouts under effective siege, but the local population was under duress. It was a similar dynamic to British soldiers who were garrisoned in homes in the American Colonies before the Revolution—the locals weren't exactly happy about feeding and housing foreign fighters. They didn't share their zeal for jihad.

The Cavalry Scouts had lost men and vehicles on several patrols and were on the ragged edge of still being an effective fighting force. Now the fighting season was coming on strong, and this FOB was in danger of being overrun—a bad way to start the summer campaign.

Mac and I knew our Rangers were the only ones who could help these guys and keep them from being overwhelmed by the IMU. The United States was transitioning power to the Afghan government, and we were already reducing troop numbers from their surge levels in anticipation of our 2014 exit deadline. There were no other options—we were it.

A couple of privates were dispatched to track down the rest of the Rangers, who were eating and doing their daily physical training before our scheduled intel brief. Those of us in the TOC, mostly the senior leaders, started making maps and analyzing significant enemy activity in the area. We weren't in our own backyard but in the IMU's, and it had been that way for most of the war in this part of Afghanistan. We couldn't augment the Cavalry Scouts, and they were too banged-up from fighting to do it themselves. We were going to have to do this old school, on foot and at night.

The immediate area around the FOB likely had only a few hundred IMU fighters. They couldn't garrison large numbers of fighters in the area because we could take them out with drones. As odd as it sounds, the dirigible over the Cavalry Scouts' FOB was a deterrent; the enemy knew we could see them, so they generally moved in small units to try to blend in as locals.

We might ultimately have to face a thousand fanatical Uzbeks whose sole purpose in life was to kill us on their way to Paradise, but it would be in squad, platoon, or, at best, company-size elements. If we were cut off, got bogged down, lost momentum, or took too many casualties, we would be overrun. It was simple math—we couldn't let the trickle of fighters become a tsunami.

This was doubly important because we had no backup. The closest Marines, Rangers, or Army infantry were at best an hour away, and they would be flying into what was already a no-fly zone. We knew the Cavalry Scouts would do all they could to get their guns into the fight, but they'd been attrited and whittled down to just a shadow of what they'd been when they set up the FOB. Any force they launched to help us out would be likely to take massive casualties, so we didn't even brief that as a contingency. I had read *Gates of Fire*, the story of the 300 Spartans who fought and died at Thermopylae, when I was in the midst of the Ranger Selection process, and that certainly came to mind as we were planning for this mission.

Simply put, our plan was to use our Ranger unit as bait to lure the IMU fighters out of the villages surrounding the FOB. Only by presenting an inviting target would they come out in large enough numbers. Any Army private knows that this is a tactic usually eschewed in favor of following a more straightforward infantry doctrine, particularly in contemporary wars waged by superpowers with high-tech weapons. But there was no other way if we wanted to kill enough Uzbeks to provide relief for the Cavalry Scouts.

As our briefing evolved, Mac and I agreed that this

mission was shaping up as one of the most challenging we'd ever faced. Once we'd landed inside the FOB and linked up with the Cavalry Scouts, the plan was for us to head for a medium-size village about 15 klicks south of the FOB. We'd pass through some smaller villages on the way and would have to clear parts of them, but the farthest village was where our intel told us the IMU units might be massing.

The terrain was the worst you could imagine. It was low ground, and there was a ravine we would have to cross to get to the main village. It was about 30 feet deep and ran north-south and just to the west of the village. If the enemy caught us while we were trying to cross the ravine, it would mean certain death. To the east were cliffs, all of them several hundred feet tall. They weren't sheer, but trying to make an ascent up those cliffs during a firefight would mean certain death as well.

The only option left to 2nd Platoon was to walk out of the FOB west-southwest a few klicks to the nearest village and clear it. We'd have to do that slowly, as we'd be following a vehicle route that had likely been mined with IEDs. Then we'd need to head almost due south, through marshes and agricultural fields, to the main village, about 10 klicks due south.

If we encountered stiff resistance we could fight our way out to the south, but that took us away from the FOB and we could easily be enveloped by a large force. The Cavalry Scouts were in no shape to rescue us. That meant

we'd have little option but to work our way back to the FOB
the way we came. That was dangerous for a number of reasons, one of which was that the enemy would have most of
the night to mine the route with IEDs, and the other of
which was that the route cut through a dense village we
knew held enemy fighters.

We also knew those fighters would be ready, as we
planned to stir up a hornet's nest as we moved through it
on our way south. As we planned our movement back to
the FOB, it looked like we'd have to cut straight through the
crop fields on our way north. But that still meant we had a
village to the left and cliffs to the right, and just-tilled soil
or the odd irrigation trench for cover. There were just no
good answers.

We were going to make this a two-platoon assault.
Both platoons would bring backup machine guns as well
as every extra 60-mm mortar cannon we had, and 1st Platoon would bring our heavy machine guns. Mac and Hank
both brought their Mk-13s.

As for 1st Platoon, their orders were to infil to the east
after we left from the FOB at night, but only after 2nd Platoon started waking people up as we moved through the
small village nearest to us. That would mask their movement as they moved south to the cliffs over barren ground.
Then they would turn south away from our area of operation and would scale the cliffs I mentioned earlier. They
would remain concealed in these cliffs until 2nd Platoon
was decisively engaged—which meant pinned down and

cut off by the enemy we'd enticed out of the main village. Then, if the plan worked the way it had been sketched out, 1st Platoon would provide a counterpunch of machine-gun fire effective enough for us to fight our way out. It was basically the opposite of any sound military doctrine I had ever heard of. On its surface, it was more like something a first-year West Point cadet would dream up after reading *Sun Tzu for Dummies*.

While I've painted this in stark, I-can't-believe-we're-doing-this terms, Team Merrill's mission was to engage our enemy in Afghanistan, and this plan was going to do it—in spades. Major Dan laid out the plan, and while dangerous, it made more and more sense. It also reminded me that getting into the fight was just what Miss America and I came to Afghanistan to do.

As soon as the briefing was finished, we got our kit and weapons together and prepared to move out. The 1st Platoon added pouches and spare barrels for our machine guns. There was a good reason for doing this.

During a sustained rate of fire, machine gun barrels literally melt through the rifling, eventually getting so hot that they glow red and begin to droop. Before this happens, we swap them out for a "cold," or spare, barrel. We were going to need them. It seems counterintuitive, but even though we were fatigued from fighting our way through long, grueling operations, the danger of this mission, and the chance to keep those Cavalry Scouts from being overrun, buoyed our spirits.

We moved to the airfield at dusk. We waited in an empty helicopter maintenance bay while the helos, which were on the other side of the airfield, finished their flight checks and taxied to us. It was going to be a long flight, so we made sure all our gear was powered down. We also knew we needed to get some sleep during the flight. The plan was for us to fight all night and sleep in the besieged FOB the following day.

As soon as the birds were in front of us, we lined up by chalk and marched into the belly of the beast. In the same way it hit me on other missions, now I knew the die was cast. I sank into my cargo-net seat, popped some foamies into my ears, and tried to get some sleep. If we made it into the FOB without getting shot down I would need it.

"FIVE MINUTES!" I awoke to the collectively echoed shout. The bird's engines were screaming full out, and the pilots were flying low, banking with the terrain. There were reports that the enemy had SAFIRE capabilities—surface-to-air-capable rockets, typically Stinger missiles left over from the days when we armed the Afghan Mujahedeen to fight the Russians—and the thought made my skin crawl.

"TWO MINUTES!" Everyone echoed Platoon Sergeant Pack's time hack, including me. I was gulping air and forcing myself to breathe out through my nose, trying to rein in the rush I felt. I had no clear thoughts yet, since, like most of the others, I had just awakened from a dead sleep, and the surge of adrenaline was just setting in.

"THIRTY SECONDS!" came the call, and it was echoed

by all of us over the screaming noise and vibrations of the Chinook's engines. The National Guard pilots never let off the throttle, and the aircrew members swiveled in their gunports searching for the attack we felt was all but guaranteed. I had only one thought: *Don't let me die on the bird.* Too many good men—and women—had died in Iraq and Afghanistan when a cheap, Cold War-era weapon like an RPG had taken down a multimillion-dollar helicopter and killed all aboard.

If I'm painting a scary picture of almost every one of the scores of helo flights I took during my six rotations to Afghanistan, it's because I intend to. Every one of them was that hazardous. I wasn't especially religious, but just in case, I hoped the Vikings were right and that if I died fighting I would go straight to Valhalla.

The "THIRTY SECONDS!" call was still resonating when suddenly the Chinooks banked into a power slide and we lurched inside the cargo hold of the bird, straining at the limits of our safety tethers. I traced my tether down to the D-Ring that was snapped onto the steel deck, wanting to ensure I was made fast to *something* so I wouldn't get thrown around the inside of the Chinook like a rag doll.

The power slide—skidding sideways—was bad enough, but then we seemed to drop out of the sky like a safe. I felt my stomach in my throat and sensed my eyes bug out from the g-force. One thought took over my brain: *This is it, we're all gonna die.*

I was bracing myself for what I knew was going to be a fiery crash when the Chinook alighted softly on the small helipad. We unsnapped our safety tethers and rushed to the helo's ramp in a chaotic press of Rangers. The Chinook was gone as soon as the last man's boots hit the ground. I finally took a breath. We cleared the small helipad and pressed against the HESCO barriers. We watched the second Chinook unload the rest of 2nd Platoon in the same way.

I looked for my sniper teammate, Marc, and saw him adjusting his night-vision goggles before he spotted me.

"Holy shit, these National Guard guys are cowboys!" he said excitedly as he trotted over to me to clap me on the shoulder. He had a big grin, and that didn't surprise me. Of course Marc would like that wild ride—he was an adrenaline junkie if there ever was one. I didn't know if he was brave or foolhardy or both, but he wasn't scared. I thought, *If we're going to die, at least my partner isn't upset about it.*

"I didn't know you could power slide in a Chinook," was all I managed to say before I heard a crackle of static on the radio. It was Platoon Sergeant Pack in my ear telling the platoon to follow him. A liaison from the Cavalry Scouts—one of only a handful of people who knew we were coming—had met us at the helo pad. The FOB was completely blacked out to discourage night mortar and rocket attacks. We picked our way through the tents and bombed-out vehicles toward the front gate of the FOB.

"Two-One lead, out," Platoon Sergeant Pack said in a hushed tone as he gestured in the direction of the gate with an IR laser. The rest of us waited until the element we were supposed to follow moved past us and fell in behind them. The IED threat was high, and our EOD man insisted on leading the way. I fell in with the squad right behind him.

Sergeant Reggie and Staff Sergeant Josh walked up to the gate of the FOB and were met by two Cavalry Scouts soldiers guarding the entrance.

"Hey, who are you guys?" one of the Cavalry Scouts guards, a private, asked.

"Never mind, Private," the trooper who must be the Sergeant of the Guard responded as he stared down Reggie and Josh. "Where do you think you're going?"

"We're going *out there*," Reggie replied curtly, pointing through the metal gate with his gloved finger. This happened a lot when we walked out of FOBs at night. The gate guards had to keep people out, but sometimes people wandered to the front gate by mistake. They just usually didn't wander out at night with night-vision goggles and an entire platoon behind them.

"It's okay. We need you to open the gate. We're conducting a patrol," Staff Sergeant Josh began calmly. "Go ahead and call back to your HQ. Your sergeant major knows about it." He looked at the guard, waiting for him to act. Staff Sergeant Josh was always cool under pressure, whereas Sergeant Reggie was practically humming with energy. Reggie was walking point, and out of all of us, he was the most pumped up for a fight.

"Okay, okay. He told me someone might be going out," the Sergeant of the Guard said to Reggie, who looked ready to pounce on him.

They opened the gate, and as we passed by I could hear them calling their HQ to make sure they hadn't just messed up and let someone out they shouldn't have.

Outside of the walls of the FOB, the light from the stars was more diffuse, and we could see well into the night. In fact, we were higher than the distant village we planned to bait the enemy into. I shouldered Miss America to look at the village in my scope. I could just make out a couple of electric lights. It was 10 klicks as the crow flies, but we were going to follow the arc of the MSR and make several stops along the way. That would turn our movement into closer to 12 klicks.

The Cavalry Scouts had been ambushed from a building in the village closest to them, just to the west. That was our first stop. We headed there as quickly as we dared and trusted our EOD man and our K-9 team to clear the way by detecting the IEDs we were certain we were walking toward.

We got to the village without incident, and as we walked through it, we didn't hear a peep. It reminded me of the Taliban-controlled neighborhood we encountered outside of Kandahar. My first thought was, *The locals must really be under the IMU's thumb.* We got to the biggest adobe building in the village and found it abandoned. Our EOD man poked around a bit with Sergeant Reggie's team, but all they found was some expended brass rifle cartridges. So far, so good.

I half expected the trip out of the village to be like walking through the bad end of a shooting gallery. I had moved out in front, closer to the distant village that was our next destination. I scanned and scanned until Sergeant Reggie and Staff Sergeant Josh walked past me, resuming our movement south. We made good progress over the open ground, and soon I could see the ravine next to the tangle of adobe buildings that made up the village. We knew from the images we had gotten from the dirigible floating above their FOB that some of the compounds likely held enemy fighters.

We paused about 50 meters west of this village so we could set up our outer cordon. That done, we quickly started clearing one compound after another as surreptitiously as we could. We entered a compound, woke up the residents, and questioned them in hushed voices, trying to get information as to where the IMU fighters might be hiding. We needed to work our way from the north side of the village, closest to the FOB, to the south side before dawn, or else our plan wasn't going to work. So there was a huge tactical reason for our hurrying.

If the IMU attacked us at night, there was zero chance they would attack en masse, and we would make quick work of them. But come dawn, if we were still in the tangle of buildings in this village, we would be fighting team by team, building to building, working our way through narrow footpaths and adobe walls that formed a maze we hadn't been able to see on our overhead maps. Add the massed fire of a determined enemy, and those mazes would turn into death traps. It was our worst-case scenario.

I covered the west side of the village, near the ravine. Marc was on the east side, backed up against the cliffs. We climbed up and down ladders and outside stairways, moving from rooftop to rooftop, looking for the best vantage points to provide overwatch and following the assault force as it moved through the village.

Inside each small courtyard, Major Dan and First Sergeant Hutch were having Zeke ask the usual questions, "Where is the Taliban?" "Can you tell them to come and fight us?" When the questioning was over, the villagers were given strict warnings to stay in their homes until we left the following day. I didn't like the fact that we were telling them our timeline, but as I said earlier, we were here for a fight, and this was certain to cause one.

It took us most of the night to clear almost all of the living quarters in the village, and now the sun was coming up. We were scattered throughout the village, except for a skeleton crew manning the outer cordon. From the enemy's perspective, it looked like a small scouting party was poking around the outskirts of the village. The rest of us were concealed inside whatever buildings we found that were built well enough to stop bullets and also had windows to shoot from.

Things were status quo in the village for the moment. We were the bait, and we were waiting for the Uzbek fighters to make their move.

Since we were in the northern part of Afghanistan and we'd begun our mission at night, we had on extra layers of clothing to stay warm. I was co-located in an adobe building with our AT (Anti-Tank) crew, the guys tasked with carrying our RAWS. My roomies were Sergeant B and his private, Skinny Pete. The sun was about to rise, and I knew it was going to get warm in a hurry.

I turned to Sergeant B and said, "I've got to get out of these layers or I'll cook today." That sounded simple enough, but it meant I would have to take off all my body armor and most of my uniform, so I wouldn't be able to monitor my radio, which was like being blind.

More unnerving, especially since we were deep in IMU territory, I wouldn't be able to put Miss America into action quickly. I was completely vulnerable. Sergeant B and I had been together at RIP (Ranger Indoctrination Program), which meant we had an extra bond of trust.

"Me and Pete will hold it down, brother, I'll let you know if we get any calls," Sergeant B replied, smiling. He was a big, cheerful guy with a barrel chest and was from Texas, so he had that larger-than-life presence.

Skinny Pete was just the opposite. He looked like Sergeant B could use him for a toothpick. They were an odd couple, but they were fearless, and we had found ourselves charging into ambushes together more than once.

"I'm going to camo up and stow my night gear. Don't kill anyone without me," I said as I ducked into a small outbuilding. I hurriedly got undressed and got ready for the heat of the day. I reapplied my camo face paint and packed my night-vision scope and goggles in a pouch. I tied them down to a small steel D-ring looped into my body armor. I took a few long pulls of water from my Camelbak. I wasn't that thirsty, but I knew I might not have time to take another drink if the enemy hit us hard at dawn.

I was kitted back up, ready to fight, but I could feel the fatigue setting in. Climbing up and down buildings wearing over 100 pounds of gear all night takes it out of you, especially after the long, fast march we made to get to the village. I finally got back with Sergeant B and Skinny Pete.

"We killed them all without you. Sorry, Sierra," Sergeant B joked. Skinny Pete laughed hard without making a sound.

I came out of the small, walled-in yard and called my sniper teammate, Marc, on the radio. Our plan was pretty fluid, so I wanted to make sure we were on the same page.

"Sierra-Three," I said, "if you haven't kitted up for daylight, you need to."

"Sierra-One, I'm all set," he piped back. Now that we were on the ground and had cleared the entirety of this village, we'd need to adjust our plans.

"Roger, I have a limited field of view here. How are you looking?" he asked. Marc was on the east side of the village and would be able to see less than I would.

"I can't see much unless I climb maybe a hundred meters," I replied. We were on low ground with another village, about 800 meters to the south. Marc was at even more of a disadvantage in seeing the larger village to our south.

"Got it," Marc replied.

"Roger, don't climb until they attack. They can't see us yet," I told him. I didn't want our big rifles to give us away as prime targets. Enemy snipers love to kill a guy with a specialty weapon, and supposedly there was still a bounty on American snipers. I really wanted Marc to go home and live his life. We may have been bait here, but I wanted him to get out more than I wanted to get out myself.

I switched to 1st Platoon's net to connect with Mac, who was hiding out of sight on the cliffs to our east.

"See anything up there?" I asked.

"Negative. We have movers and motos . . . too far for PID," Mac replied, calm as could be. He was referring to "positive identification," something we always had to do before opening fire on anyone. If our plan worked, he would have free rein over 1,500 meters. Mac was in the perfect spot. From his elevated position, he had nothing but air between him and any target that presented itself.

People were meandering toward us in a way that seemed random but was actually a tactic we were familiar with.

Since we were bait, all we could do was wait. We were well hidden in the tangle of buildings—we weren't about to let enemy snipers pick us off—and we wanted to make them mass and come at us. I tried to remember what building number each Ranger element was in but found it impossible. We were spread out and broken down in buddy teams and fire teams.

The sun had been fully up for almost an hour, but

nothing had happened yet. Our flight of Kiowa birds had exhausted their mission time and had to go off-station. That meant we were going to be on our own for a while. I got a sinking feeling in my stomach as the Kiowas made a final pass and headed out over the mountains.

Suddenly, the radios came alive. "All elements of 2nd Platoon, grab your kit and prep for exfil." It was Platoon Sergeant Pack. We had mapped out preplanned positions where we would consolidate and move out. Our platoon started climbing out of rooftop hides and windows where they had maintained firing positions. Those of us already at the perimeter continued to pull security, and soon we were joined by the rest of the platoon.

I knew that I needed to cover the exfil, and I called Marc. "You have the east side of the village, so when we exfil, you pick up rear. I'll head out with the lead squad on the west side so I can cover the village we passed on the way in."

"Roger that," Marc keyed back. He spoke in a monotone, and I assumed he must be as tired as I was.

"And Marc, don't let anyone come up on our six," I instructed. ("On your six" means directly behind you, at the "six o'clock" position.) "You pull rear and zap anyone trying to chase us down."

"You got it," Marc replied. Marc always seemed casual, but he was as serious a fighter as I've ever worked with. I had Marc pulling rear, which leveraged his ability to see and fire at an enemy as far as a klick away.

I looked north, back in the direction of the FOB. It was

13 klicks away. To get there, we'd have to work our way through tilled fields, and it was getting hotter by the minute.

As the platoon began its exfil, I got up from my kneeling position. Sergeant Ryan, the Alpha Team Leader, who was right next to me, got up too. Suddenly, machine-gun bullets zipped over our heads.

Ryan and I hit the dirt, along with the rest of the team. We could hear PKM machine guns cranking away at us from four or five positions. In between PKM bursts, AK-47s opened up from a number of different directions. We could tell from the sound of the shots that the enemy was firing from the extreme range of their weapons, so the bullets were hitting in wide, unpredictable swaths.

We could hear them getting closer as the sound of their guns grew louder. At the same time, their volume of fire intensified. We were returning fire and slowing them, but they were gaining ground. We watched with growing concern as the Uzbeks began flanking us. If they succeeded, we'd be pinned against the cliffs and picked off.

Ryan pointed to a goat path that looked like a passage to the other side of the ravine I had wanted to avoid. I nodded, and he signaled his fire team. We dashed down the narrow path, half sliding at times, then churned our legs like pistons climbing up the other side. We found a bit of micro-terrain, a little wrinkle of a low spot, that would provide a bit of cover for about 100 meters as we worked our way closer to the enemy.

Ryan and I hit the dirt and low-crawled until a machine gun opened up on us. The rounds were several feet over our head. We both took aim at the muzzle flashes. Ryan jammed out five or six rounds, and I sent three rounds at the flashing machine gun. Our shots were on target and that gun went silent.

The rest of Ryan's team was lined up a few meters to our left, firing at the enemy machine guns. Ryan added his fire, and another machine gun went quiet. I looked left, about 350 meters away, and spotted a small walled-in compound. I could see a man talking into a radio. I zoomed from 6 to 10 power on my scope. This guy didn't have a weapon. He put his radio in his vest and looked in the direction of our attackers. Suddenly another machine gun burst zipped over our heads.

Ryan's fire team returned fire, and the enemy machine gun went silent.

The man pulled out the radio again and looked back toward us. I knew what he was doing and figured that mortars would be next. If I let him call them in, we were going to be carrying casualties back under fire.

I could hear the rest of the platoon taking a beating from machine-gun fire coming from the enemy south of the village. I rechecked the range to our enemy spotter. He was right at 350 meters. Miss America was "zeroed," meaning "set dead on" for three hundred meters, so I needed to aim slightly higher to match my point of impact to my point of aim. I squeezed off a single round. I looked through my scope and watched the man crumple. It was like he was a puppet and I had cut his strings.

I scanned behind him, looking for other Uzbeks who might be backing him up. I saw a woman on her hands and knees at the door of the mud hut that must have been his home. I scanned the rest of the compound, but there was nothing there.

Meanwhile, the Uzbek fighters had moved in for the kill, coming to within a few hundred meters of us—just where we wanted them. Then I heard the sound of a dozen M240 machine guns go cyclic. 1st Platoon was opening up on the enemy with all they had. The noise of the M240s echoed off the cliffs where 1st Platoon was laid up and drowned out the disjointed noise of the enemy weapons.

They began alternating their fire—"talking the guns," as we call it. This means that one machine gunner fires a long burst and the machine gunner next to him starts up before, or immediately when, the first gun stops. In this way there is continuous machine-gun fire, although the two guns are alternating their fire. This prolongs our ability to maintain a cyclic rate of fire. This nonstop stream of machine-gun fire silenced the enemy. (Fire coming from such an elevated position is called "plunging fire," since it falls in an arc toward the enemy.)

The radios came alive with a commanding voice. It was Platoon Sergeant Pack, and his call was insistent: "All right, 2nd Platoon, let's move out while they have us covered."

"Two-One lead out, all elements send me your ups," Pack continued, telling us to report in with casualties and the status of our gear. It's what we do each time to ensure we're good to go for movement out of an objective area. Our squad and team leaders ran from man to man, checking each one, making sure no casualty was missed in the adrenaline rush of what we just lived through.

"Two-One, blue sky, moving out," Staff Sergeant Josh replied as he moved into the open field and waved his men into a wedge at a brisk walk. ("Blue sky" was our term that meant we were good to go.)

"Copy," Platoon Sergeant Pack replied.

Then came the calls of the other team leads: "Two-Two, blue sky," "Two-Three, blue sky." We were now out in the open field. We had about 500 meters to go before 1st Platoon would no longer be able to cover us from their position in the cliffs.

"Sierra, blue sky," I finally called and headed out. I was about midway through our formation, which was now moving at a fast trot. We had maximum dispersal of about 15 to 20 meters between each man. We were paralleling the MSR we had walked along the night before. There were clusters of motos with double and triple riders. They were following us, and they were trying to find a path to get to us.

My earpiece came alive. "BREAK, BREAK, BREAK, 1st Platoon is breaking down, we are on our own," came the call over the net. We now had steep hills on our right and a village full of IMU on our left. 1st Platoon's fires were masked by the steep little mountains between us, and they broke down their position and exfiled. Mac told me later that they ran a more direct route back to the FOB.

About 100 away, at the head of the formation, I watched Sergeant Bob motion and heard his voice in my earpiece.

"Sierra," he breathed heavily into his mic. "We've got a moto gang. Can you get eyes?"

"Roger," was all the breath I had to answer him as I put my long, heavy gun over my shoulder and started sprinting. I got to Sergeant Bob, who hadn't slowed a bit, and dropped to a knee. A quick count of the motos told me we had fifteen of them. Worse, they were in a good ambush spot. Worse still, they were smart: they had no visible weapons. I sent a round toward them and it splashed in front of the moto driver who seemed to be in the lead. They kicked their bikes in a circle.

"Warning shot, no weapons," I called breathlessly across the net. I heard a static, breathless "Copy" from somewhere in the formation.

"BREAK. Sierra, we've got some motos coming up behind us, seven o'clock."

I keyed back "Copy."

I turned around and started running back the way I came. I needed to move toward the rear of the formation to scope out the threat and engage if possible. A Ranger Sniper's job is also to be a skirmisher and to keep the enemy occupied. We did that at a distance with our sniper fire while the rest of the platoon moved out.

I saw another group of motos trying to follow a rough path toward us. I looked back along our column and saw Mark taking aim at them. He sent a couple of warning shots their way, and they wheeled back the way they came.

I got up and started running again, this time forward, toward the front of the formation. It was my job to skirmish again. Using my sniper scope, I could clear the way ahead while the rest of the platoon kept on moving. My area of responsibility was the front and west side, Marc's was the back and west side, and we met in the middle.

"Sierra-One, Two-One." Sergeant Reggie's voice came across the net, calm as could be. "We have another moto gang. It looks like they're blocking us from the FOB."

Leave it to Reggie to not be out of breath. I picked up my pace and ran past the trotting Rangers. I could see a shine in front of me, which turned out to be water. Soon I was splashing through a flooded wheat field, like a shallow rice paddy. The mud sucked at my boots, and I pumped hard, trying to catch up with the lead squad.

"Sierra, we have guys at our nine o'clock," I heard over the radio from a team leader in the trail squad.

"That's you, Marc," I panted into my mic.

"On it," Marc called back. At this point, none of us had enough breath for formality.

I caught up with the first squad. We were about 350 meters from the moto gang that was blocking our way back to the FOB. There were maybe two dozen bikes, but with each of them having two or three riders, they were close to matching us man for man. I dropped to a knee and shouldered my rifle. I looked through my scope and tried to spot weapons. But for some reason they just revved up and took off in every direction away from us.

"Any weapons, Sierra?" Sergeant Reggie asked.

"No, nothing," I replied. I was disappointed but also relieved. We popped up, and Reggie sprinted back to his team. They had never slowed down. I fell into pace with the squad next to me.

We ran as a platoon the whole time, slogging through the flooded fields and furrowed fields toward the FOB. Marc and I were running up and down the length of the platoon, but this was a running firefight, so we had to sprint to a crisis point, forward or behind. But as soon as a crisis was averted, we had to run back to our position in formation. In my case this was somewhere about parallel or behind the lead element; in Marc's case, somewhere in the trailing third of the formation. This entire movement took well over an hour before the FOB came into sight.

We trotted the last quarter mile before pumping hard up the hill into the open gates of the FOB. We all straightened up under our heavy kit and began breathing as evenly and calmly as we could. We did this mainly because right outside the FOB was a dangerous place to linger, but partly because there were other soldiers inside those gates who were watching us. I don't think we could control the look on our faces.

We were tired, haggard, and pumped full of adrenaline.

There were Cavalry Scout soldiers on both sides of the small road just inside the gates of the FOB, about a dozen on each side. It seems word had gotten around the small camp about just what we were doing. Those Cavalry Scouts were out of Army food, but they had care packages their loved ones had sent them with their favorite snacks and comfort food. They had gathered up several boxes of this and gave them to us as we came in, along with bottles of water. It was grab-and-go, and we exchanged a few quick handshakes and thank you's as we kept pushing farther inside the walls to make room for the Rangers behind us. We all had to get through those gates to safety before our mission could be called a success.

Once we were all inside the FOB, we headed to a bombed-out vehicle bay. It offered overhead cover and a little bit of shade. It had been patched up with plywood, chain-link fencing, and sandbags, so at least we would have a proper burial if we got blown up by rockets and mortars. We stretched out, using our body armor and Camelbaks as pillows. If the guys we fought earlier regrouped and attacked the FOB, the Cavalry Scouts were going to get their chance to show them some American foreign policy. Task Force Merrill was out like a light in a matter of minutes.

We woke up about an hour before dusk and got our intelligence dump. We had a satellite feed, so there was no reason not to hear what the day's intel had generated. For this intel dump, we had the benefit of hearing intercepted enemy communications. What we heard cheered us beyond words.

We had killed almost fifty IMU fighters and had wounded even more. Out here in the remote northern wastes of Afghanistan, most of those wounded were doomed as well. There was more good news—no civilian casualties were reported.

We waited through dusk and into the early darkness of night. We were silent and tired, but also pumped about our victory over the IMU. Finally, when it was fully dark, our 160th SOAR brothers, along with several National Guard Chinooks, came thundering our way to take us back to Mazar-i-Sharif.

When we got back to MES it was creeping up on dawn. We had to drag ourselves from the airfield to our tents, but no one was watching us now, and we didn't try to hide how completely exhausted we were.

With practiced motions we sat on our bunks and re-habbed our kits. We cleaned the dust from our guns and night-vision gear. We reloaded our magazines, checking each one for damage. Some had bullet holes, some were crushed, and some were cracked. We put new batteries in our electronics and stuffed snacks into the few pockets that didn't have mission-critical items. Our movements were automatic, free of thought. We might as well have been automatons.

Once we got our gear squared away we knew we needed to get some shut-eye. We had just 8 hours before the next intel dump and planning session. We'd already been told we'd be going on another mission as soon as dark-ness fell.

This wasn't a classic mission where we planned things out and executed the plan. It was more like getting attacked by muggers in an alley and fighting your way out. But it had accomplished two things: it gave the Cavalry Scouts some badly needed breathing room to resume juras with the local elders and it pushed the enemy back long enough that the Cavalry Scouts' FOB could be resupplied.

6

CASTLE MISSION

Our mission to rescue the Cavalry Scouts had been challenging, and it was amazing we completed that effort without any of our Rangers getting killed or wounded. Just as we had done when we were operating out of Kandahar, we were constantly working to "build the picture" of the battle space. That meant that during every mission we conducted we learned more about the area's geography, more about how little control the Afghan government had in the area, more about the enemy, and, most important, more about the capabilities of our Ranger unit.

You might think that all Rangers who complete the tough selection and training process are pretty much carbon copies of each other. But it isn't until you get into combat that you really find out how long a man can march with a hundred-pound pack, how well he performs under pressure, or even how long a shot a sniper can take with a good probability of taking down a target. We'd already answered a lot of those questions in the several months of this rotation to Afghanistan, and we were about to answer more of them on this mission.

Word spread around our little tent city that we had an emergent mission and we'd be called into TOC that evening for an intel brief. That meant we all had to focus on getting our kit together, gathering our weapons and ammo, and doing whatever else was needed to prepare to launch that evening. I got together my sniper gear, and even before our intel brief, Marc and I started sorting out our roles and responsibilities for this mission.

The intel brief in TOC was pretty straightforward. Afghans in several villages in the same province as our last mission were under the thumb of the IMU. The villagers were tolerating it because they really didn't have much choice.

Because our intelligence told us there was such a heavy IMU presence in these villages, our higher headquarters thought this presented another opportunity for us to do what we do best—serve as bait to draw the Uzbek terrorists to us and then kill as many of them as we possibly could. We had done this sort of mission so many times that we'd even moved beyond the gallows humor of "here we go again, we're like cheese for a hungry mouse," and shrugged it off as just another mission.

We launched out of our base at Mazar-i-Sharif and headed northeast to Kunduz Province. It was a short flight, and I was already into my mental and physical "zone" as our Chinooks pounded through the night sky, Miss America resting in my lap. Marc and I had already tightened up our plans, and we knew we'd be providing overwatch for our Ranger assault force as they swept through the villages.

We landed about 10 klicks from the first target village and headed for it at a brisk pace. We stuck to the low ground between rolling hills until we hit a hard-packed dirt road. This area was no-man's-land—there were no Afghan army or coalition bases nearby, no government patrols, no government activity at all. The good news was that there was also virtually no IED threat, so we made good time over the ground.

We reached the target village, and Marc and I paused at a short stone wall while the rest of the platoon set up an outer cordon to the north and south to effectively surround the village. Marc and I were setting up to do our normal overwatch when suddenly we heard a disorganized smattering of full-auto AK-47 fire to the south of our position.

"Let's go, Marc!" I half-shouted, eager to get into the fight.

Before I could get off a knee and begin to move south to get our guns in the fight, we heard more AK-47 fire to the north. The volume of fire made it clear that there were more than a few fighters taking on our platoon.

"Wait!" I shouted at Marc as I grabbed him by the shoulder strap of his kit. I was trying to get us both to be still so we could listen for where the enemy fire was most intense, since that's where we'd be needed the most.

Suddenly we heard more AK fire on full auto, but this time from the west. Now we were all but surrounded.

I flashed back to our intel briefing and our strategy to use our platoon as bait. I guess that part was working, but maybe too well.

I didn't have to sort out the radio chatter to understand how we were responding. Our weapons squad leader was a bit south of where Marc and I had set up our overwatch position, and we could hear the sound of our Ranger weapons—SAW-249s and M240 machine guns—going full cyclic, pouring out a withering amount of fire. The enemy had a machine gun in the fight, but our weapons were drowning it out.

My radio came alive, and I could hear the platoon sergeants directing the fight. Our massed fire was driving the enemy west, around the village and into the mountains.

I heard Platoon Sergeant Pack's voice on the radio. He was to the north with Third Squad, and the fighting there sounded just as intense.

I could see the agitation in Marc's face. Our Ranger buddies were engaged on three fronts by a determined enemy. He wanted to get our guns into the fight.

"What are we doing, man?" he asked.

I quickly assessed the tactical situation. I had a dense, uncleared village to move through to get to the Two-Four Squad to the southwest, and I'd probably be in their line of fire—a small probability, but too great a risk. I would have to circle back around and come from behind to link up with our forces to the north, but that would take too long and would put us on low ground behind them.

"It's no good," I replied.

Marc just stared at me in disbelief. My head was swiveling, trying to gauge where the enemy was and figure out the best way to get to them.

"We'll go right up the middle," I said. "There's a bit of high ground clear of buildings near the center of the village. We can skirt to the north and avoid the densest part of the village. We should be able to see both ends of the fight from there."

"What the fuck!" Marc exclaimed. "We're surrounded and you want to walk through this village alone?" I could tell by the look on his face that he thought my plan could get us killed and not do a damn thing to protect our assault team.

He wasn't wrong, but playing it safe didn't fit my playbook. Marc was thinking of us as two snipers, while I was thinking of us as two guys with giant M4s. It wasn't the first time we had disagreed about how to roll the dice.

"Fuck it, then," I said angrily. I turned my back on Marc and headed into the village.

Just then, from behind me, Sergeant B, our RAWS gunner from Texas, piped up.

"Me and Skinny Pete will come with you, Balls!" he shouted. With Sergeant B it was never a request; it was more of a statement of what he was going to do.

With Sergeant B and his private, that made us a fire team. I gave Sergeant B and Marc a nod and kept walking.

I was ahead of them, and I was the ranking member, so I just kept moving. It was on them to catch up with me; I was setting the pace.

I made it about five steps down my path when a small figure darted out of the shadows onto the hard-packed footpath I was taking. The figure was wearing a burka, and I immediately saw that it was holding something close to its chest. I stopped cold.

Was this a suicide bomber with a mortar or a rocket rigged to blow? Or was this a mother and her infant fleeing from the chaos that had erupted around them? I was in the perfect place for a suicide bomber's attack at the center of our lines while our forces were decisively engaged on two fronts. It was a classic divide-and-conquer move, and it was coming at me full speed.

My mind computed variables at hyper-speed. If I took a shot to stop this person from detonating a bomb, I couldn't risk a head shot. Heads bob and move more than any other part of the body. I only had time for one shot, and it had to shut down the central nervous system instantly or the bomber would still be able to detonate an IED. My best bet was to shoot high in the chest, splitting the difference between the heart and the spine. At this distance, the sheer velocity should disrupt both and drop the person like a stone. It also meant I had to shoot through whatever the bomber was carrying.

A little more than 20 meters behind me, still partially covered by low stone walls, were Marc and our AT team. Any repurposed ordnance this Afghan figure was carrying would only kill me. The boys would get some overpressure, but they would live.

My decision became immediately clear: I was here to watch over my buddies, not for self-preservation.

My visible red laser danced on the figure's chest for an instant. Clenching the teeth I expected to be flying through the back of my head, I took up all the slack in my trigger as I lowered my rifle barrel to fire at the dirt between me and the sprinting Afghan. The bullet kicked up dust, causing an immediate reaction. The figure turned 90 degrees and darted into a skinny gap in the adobe wall to my left. I saw the profile and knew I had made the right call: it was a woman, and the bundle in her arms was indeed a child.

I breathed the biggest breath of my life and continued to trot toward the center of the village.

We made it to the clearing on the high ground, and the sound of Soviet-era guns was getting quieter, which was a good sign. It meant that our Rangers to the southeast were chasing the enemy they hadn't killed into the foothills of the Hindu Kush.

Marc and I could see the lasers from our Rangers on the assault team chasing man-shaped shadows before they stumbled and fell. Some of those figures faltered but continued to scrabble into the hills.

"I'm on these guys," Marc said hurriedly as he stroked his green IR laser around the shadows.

"Roger, watch your FLOT. I've got eyes right," I replied. FLOT is "front line trace," in this case the muzzle flashes of our friendly forces.

We were both tach'd out, meaning redline on a tachometer. We were maxed out, winded, oxygen-starved, and in danger of making bad decisions or having important things slip. It seems simple, but watching the FLOT means making damn sure you didn't shoot at the muzzle flashes coming from your fellow Rangers' guns.

I glanced at the area Marc was lazing and then shifted focus and turned my attention to the north, where the rest of our Rangers were hammering away at the enemy, who by this time was returning fire weakly. Our guys had beaten them back into the low ground and one walled-in compound.

Suddenly, Marc piped up. "Balls, give me a spot. I have a mover at 900 meters."

I turned to the west and saw a faint light, as well as Marc's laser.

I turned on my flood laser to illuminate the area for Marc, but before I could shoulder my rifle, Marc had clicked his laser off and cracked off a shot.

The light—probably a phone or a small flashlight or lantern carried by Marc's target—went out.

The enemy fire had now almost ceased. They'd tried to encircle us, and, damn it, they'd almost succeeded. Now most of them were probably melting back into the mountains to the west of the village. That didn't mean the village was completely free of enemy fighters, so we proceeded cautiously.

A short time later, we had the south side of the village encircled and under Ranger control. We were still fighting through waning resistance on the north side. One of the Two-One team leaders signaled to us, and I sent Marc to link up with him. The assault squad was already piling up enemy weapons and destroying them, and was surrounding the compounds where the enemy fighters had been.

The plan was to have Marc climb to where he had a good view of the entire village and make sure we weren't reengaged by a pocket of resistance or an enemy element that had regrouped on the high ground and was going to stream down the hills and counterattack.

The firefight had died down, and the assault net was finally cleared now that we weren't maneuvering under fire. I called up the platoon sergeant, gave him our position, and let him know that I was with his AT team— Sergeant B and Skinny Pete and their antitank weapon.

"Roger, move north so they can support us, and keep an eye on those hills," he replied.

Sergeant B was already heading north. I saw him moving along a wall when suddenly a giant Kuchi dog leaped to the top of an 8-foot wall and loomed over him, just a meter away.

A Kuchi, or Afghan shepherd dog, is an Afghan herding dog that takes its name from the Kuchi people of Afghanistan. It looks like a 150-pound hyena with the mane of a lion. For centuries, Afghan nomads used these Kuchis as guard and working dogs, following their caravans and flocks of sheep, goats, camels, and other livestock and protecting them from wolves, big cats, and thieves.

But the terrorists we'd come to Afghanistan to kill had

perverted the Kuchis, training them to be killers, just like their new masters. A Kuchi is easily capable of killing a man.

This nightmare of a dog had a thin lead trailing from its neck. I signaled Sergeant B with my laser.

He looked at the dog and looked back at me. "He's on a lead," he said with a smile, and then turned his back on the Kuchi and continued walking. Sergeant B was assuming the dog's lead was tied down somewhere inside the compound and was long enough to let the dog get to the top of the wall but no farther. Sadly, he was wrong.

As soon as Sergeant B turned away, the Kuchi dog leapt down from the wall without a sound. His lead trailed behind him—it was attached to nothing. Now just a few feet from Sergeant B, it crouched to leap at him.

I centered my laser on the beast and fired from the hip, sending a round through the animal's front shoulders. The huge Kuchi faltered and rolled on his back, just inches from Sergeant B. He and I nodded our lasers to each other, and the big Texan grinned.

"DOGS, DOGS, DOGS!" I called over the net so that our leadership understood that we weren't engaged by the enemy.

"Seven," our platoon sergeant keyed back, signaling his understanding.

We moved north and found a bit of rocky high ground. We watched the platoon below us working its way through several compounds, stacking up weapons they'd taken from the enemy we'd killed.

We assessed the tactical situation and realized that some of the enemy had escaped to the north. Our platoon leader called in a fire mission.

We could see four of the enemy begin climbing the hills to the north of the village, trying to escape. They were about 100 meters ahead of us. We heard Stryker, our JTAC, calling the Hercules AC-130 gunship and soon heard the roar of its four turboprop engines.

A minute later we heard the resounding boom of the Herk's 40-mm cannon. It boomed four times, and seconds later four explosions cracked the ground near the fleeing IMU. Stryker called the gunship with a firing adjustment, and we heard another dozen 40-mm rounds metered out in four-round bursts.

We never bothered to look for the bodies. That many rounds from an AC-130 literally buries people. There would be no bodies to recover and no weapons to destroy.

A minute or two after that, I was watching the hills and saw a young man creeping along the slope toward Two-Three (Sergeant John's squad). He was a MAM and was ducking and looking, slinking closer to the assault force.

"Two-Three, we've got a MAM maneuvering toward Third Squad in the high ground."

"Sierra-One, do you have PID?" the platoon leader asked me.

I watched the man crouch and work on something on the ground.

"Negative," I replied. "He's burying something right

now. Clear to engage?" I asked, putting conviction in my voice. I needed to take this guy out now.

"Negative, Sierra, you know we need PID," John replied. He knew how badly I wanted to kill this guy—hell, he wanted me to—but he had to keep me out of jail as well as alive. "Do not engage!" he commanded.

A few seconds passed as we both stewed. We knew what we needed to do to take out a guy who was clearly intent on killing us, but the damn ROE were banging up against logic.

"Sierra-One, what's he doing now?" John asked. "Give me a laze," he ordered.

I lazed the creeping man with my invisible green laser.

"He's crouching when he walks, and he just got done burying something next to this goat path," I said, urgency in my voice.

"Roger, we've got eyes on him." It was Mac. He put a laze on the guy. I saw three more, and finally five lasers sweep over the man. He couldn't see the lasers, and he could barely see us, but he kept creeping toward the assault force.

No one digs holes on the side of a mountain, and nobody sneaks up on armed soldiers if they don't have ill intentions. As a sniper, it's your job to roll the dice with your own life, not the lives of the people you overwatch.

I had Miss America's suppressor on; otherwise, a warning shot would likely send the man running, either toward us because he's enemy or away from us because he's innocent. I took aim across his hips, hoping to shatter his pelvis. That would ensure he couldn't run. If I was a little off, he would bleed out internally or die of septic shock in a day or two.

I eased back on the trigger and Miss America spit out a shell. Mac opened up on him as soon as he heard my rifle report. His squad followed suit, including their SAW gunner, and the man was dead in a hail of bullets before he hit the ground.

"Sierra-One, did you PID that EKIA?" (EKIA means "enemy killed in action.) It was our platoon sergeant. I couldn't tell if he was pissed or worried that we killed a civilian, but I could tell he wanted an answer.

"Negative," I called back, putting confidence in my voice. "He dug in a bomb and continued maneuvering on Third Squad."

"Two-Three, go search the body and find out what he was doing," Platoon Sergeant Pack called over the net, ignoring me.

"Roger, Seven," Two-Three called back. His team spread out and moved methodically toward the body. I could hear their report over the net. They didn't find any weapons. I started to get nervous. I would be investigated over this either way, and if we couldn't justify the shot I took, I could face a murder charge.

Two-Three continued on down the goat path.

"Where did you see the EKIA digging, Sierra?" Two-Three asked me.

"Three, Sierra, right here," I replied as I lassoed the spot with my laser.

"Platoon sergeant, Two-Three, we got something here. Looks like Sierra was right, he dug something in."

Our EOD man came across the net and started telling Two-Three the best way to get close enough and provide enough details to try to identify what the device at the bottom of the hole might be.

That conversation was stepped on by an urgent call from the platoon leader. "BREAK, BREAK, BREAK. The AC-130 just PIDed four enemy fighters moving to you, Two-Three. Get back to the compound. We have a fire mission inbound."

Two-Three and his squad beat feet back the way they came. Moments later, we heard the thump of the 40-mm cannon on the AC-130 ring out, followed by four corresponding explosive cracks on the opposite side of the hill that Two-Three was just on. They fired twelve more rounds in three bursts and buried the four enemy fighters and their weapons not 75 meters from the ones they had killed earlier.

The man Two-Three and I killed was spotting for the team of fighters who were going to ambush us from the high ground. If he was any good, once he finished with his spotting mission he was probably going to run back along his goat path and lead anyone who pursued them into the small mine he buried in his tracks.

We finished destroying weapons and searching the few bodies we found. We had engaged dozens of fighters, but we only found a handful of bodies. This wasn't a surprise. We knew they carried their dead and wounded away so they wouldn't fall into our hands, a reminder of the IMU's training and discipline.

That done, we formed into a loose skirmish line along the rock wall where we had all started the night before. The sun was rising, and ominous storm clouds rolled in and covered the sky.

Our AC-130 went off-station: the cloud ceiling was too low and thick for them to be effective. They were supposed to be replaced with Apache gunships, but they wouldn't do us any good. The ceiling was down to 500 feet—too low for helo ops. The only fire support we had were our own 60-mm mortars. They were faster to respond but weren't as terrorizing to the enemy as buzzing airplanes and helicopters. They always made the kind of statement that could prevent us from being attacked.

We had planned to get back to the ROD site before dawn, but we were going to have to walk down the MSR in broad daylight. The rain started to sprinkle, and I hoped this wasn't going to be one of the annual torrents that dumped buckets and lasted for two or three days.

We moved out down the road, but because of the rolling terrain, we could only see straight down the MSR. Every hundred meters or so we encountered a hill that was about 100 feet high. That kind of terrain meant that there could be an army of IMU waiting over the next hill, ready to ambush us. Without aircraft spotting for us, we would never see them coming. Our mortar men needed a forward observer to spot for them so they could shoot anything they couldn't see themselves.

"All right, Marc, this is gonna suck, we gotta run the flats and climb each hill before the platoon gets there," I said.

Marc nodded gravely, his face a reflection of the exhaustion I felt.

I drank the last couple of sips of water from my Camelbak.

"Remember, all we have are mortars," I told him. "If the shit hits the fan, you'll direct them."

"Roger that," he replied. At this stage of the mission, just speaking was an effort.

"Seven, Sierra-One," I called on the net.

"Go for, Seven," Platoon Sergeant Pack called back.

"Seven, we're going to run a relay to the hilltops and overwatch you as you move."

"Good to go, Sierra," Pack replied. "We'll send up a gun if you get in a TIC." (TIC means "troops in contact.")

It was important for Marc and me to climb those hills. Our machine gunners were carrying a massive amount of weight with their guns and would only climb those steep, loose-packed hills if absolutely necessary. We were effectively their scouts.

I took off at a sprint, passing the rest of the trotting Rangers. Every part of me was cramping. I hit the bottom of the slope at a dead sprint and pumped my knees high and hard. I held my rifle balanced on my shoulder with my right hand and clawed at the hill with my left. I paused just below the crest, then blew out hard two or three times before creeping to the pinnacle just enough to level my rifle over the top.

"Sierra, clear," I huffed into my radio.

"Sierra, moving," Marc said. He had to pull rear security, and I watched him sprint past the trotting Rangers at full tilt. Marc had always had some serious wheels, fast even by Ranger Standards. He looked like a maniac, but he hit the next rolling hill ahead of the rest of the platoon and churned up it. I watched him pause below the crest and blow out a few breaths before peeking over the hill as I had.

"Sierra, clear!" He forced the air out of his heaving chest and managed to pound out the words.

"Sierra, moving," I called back. The rest of the platoon never broke stride.

I let gravity take me down the hill, my legs barely touching the ground. I was winded, and my legs and back were screaming with lactic acid and cramps before I hit the low ground. Spittle and snot came from my nose and mouth, and my breaths were guttural sounds. The Rangers I passed were like metronomes, trotting as fast as most people run. They could keep up that pace for days. I hit the next slope and used my left arm like a gorilla, clawing my way to the top of the hill again.

We did this three more times, but we got through those hills without being ambushed by the IMU, and I think Marc and I built a lot of street cred with the rest of the platoon. I was maxed out, and I wondered if I had enough gas in the tank to fight my way out of this the following night.

As we continued north toward the ROD site, we came

upon another village, divided by a small creek. Back at MES, some Army SOF PSYOPS (psychological operations) guys had given us leaflets to distribute when we went through the villages.

The leaflets were pretty artfully done, with dramatic pictures and texts that said, in several Afghan languages, things like "Drones are watching you" and "Coalition forces are coming to kill the IMU who are oppressing you." It seemed surreal, walking through this village on a beautiful spring day just as people are waking up and handing out colorful leaflets talking about death and destruction.

We got through the village without incident. By now, the sun had burned off the clouds that had dumped rain on us just a little while ago, and we could see well ahead of us. There was our ROD compound on the top of a hill.

We'd stayed in some pretty nondescript ROD sites before, but this wasn't one of them. This was a massive compound shaped like a castle. Our two-story home was in the center, with the second story winding around like a parapet.

We were exhausted from our night mission, and once inside the ROD site we dumped our gear, set up watch rotations, and got some badly needed rack.

I pulled watch for the first part of the day, then swapped with Marc in the early afternoon and caught some rack myself. I slept on the second floor of our "castle." Remarkably for Afghanistan, it had bay windows on all four sides. As much as I reminded myself that the reason we were in Afghanistan was to kill the enemy, I thought it would be a shame if we made contact here, because the first thing those of us in the parapet would have to do would be to smash those bay windows out so we could return fire.

By the time I woke up, it was nearing dusk.

I staggered downstairs and saw that one of the guys had killed a turkey, and a group of them were roasting it on a spit.

We ate a turkey dinner—a rare treat—while we went over our plans for that night. We used stones and sticks to make a "sand table"—basically a scale model of the next village we were going to. Once we had our plan set, we spent the last of the twilight making our final preparations.

When it was completely dark we heard the unmistakable, and welcome, sound of Kiowas. That was our cue, and we moved out.

We had been ambushed and surrounded the previous night, and we barely escaped. Most of the Taliban and IMU knew not to fight Americans at night, but these guys weren't playing by that rule. Something else was at work.

We already had our intelligence group collecting information on the enemy, using the many mysterious ways they plied their craft. They told us that we had killed over forty IMU fighters the previous night and wounded many more. That was the good news. The bad news was that there were still thousands of IMU in the province. Apparently, the previous night hadn't been a knockout punch; all we had done was stir up a hornet's nest.

I didn't usually carry more than one grenade, if I carried any at all. Tonight I made sure I had four of them, and I added a couple extra magazines from our Speedball. The additional mags only gave me forty extra rounds, but I'm a sniper, so I figured, "one shot, one kill."

We streamed out of the ROD site and headed down the road toward our target village. We could hear two Kiowas approaching from the southeast, and if we could hear them, so could the enemy. We knew we wouldn't have the element of surprise tonight.

We made our way into the village. It was only about 800 meters from the ROD site. I was walking near the front with the lead squad, while Marc, as usual, was pulling rear. He was watching our trail, as well as the back half of our formation, and was moving to wherever he was needed.

We got to our first blocking position at an intersection. I took a knee along with the machine-gun team. I wanted Marc to stay with them and help discourage enemy reinforcements from the surrounding villages. I used our wait time to confirm ranges with the gun team leader. It was a well-practiced exchange by now. We sized up the terrain, and the corporal leading the gun team was getting pretty good at ranging things by eye.

Marc showed up with the trail elements of 2nd Platoon and took a knee next to me. We noticed three men walking toward a structure about 400 meters from us. Each man was carrying a wrapped bundle, and one of them had what was either a shovel or an RPG over his shoulder.

We'd been in-country long enough to know that the only thing an Afghan man would be carrying in a long wrapped bundle like that was several rifles. Worse, at that range a shovel over the shoulder looked identical to an RPG. Mac and I had learned that lesson the hard way the last time we were deployed together.

I got Marc on them with his scope and we looked at them together, manipulating our scopes, zooming in and out, fiddling with our focus rings. But before we could make out for certain what they were carrying, they were inside the building. It *did* look like an outbuilding of some kind, and it *was* the end of a workday. They could just be putting their tools away for the night. In that case they would come out empty-handed and head to their homes. But if they weren't farmers, then they'd hole up in that outbuilding if a firefight started. I was certain the latter was the case, but the ROE made the call for me.

"No PID, Marc?" I asked once they were inside. I was still scrutinizing the door they had entered.

"No, just bundles and a shovel," he replied. He was keyed up for the mission, but his relaxed tone told me he wasn't as convinced these guys were bad actors as I was.

"If they come out again and they're carrying those bundles, that means it isn't a shovel," I explained. "Just keep eyes on it. If they come out empty-handed, call it up." (That meant he should report it over the radio.) "If they come out with something over their shoulder, it's an RPG. Nobody digs holes all day and then digs holes all night."

Marc nodded without taking his eye out of his scope.

"Do a countdown with the gun and start firing at the same time, but make sure you shoot the guy with RPG first," I said, wanting us to count down from "three" and then fire at the enemy simultaneously.

"Roger, Balls," Marc replied.

"I mean it, man. Those guys come back out, you light them up," I commanded. I was so sure these guys were bad actors that I could taste it.

I got up and trotted after the rest of the platoon. I wanted to stay at the blocking position. I knew these guys were bad, and I wanted to be the one to kill them.

But Marc could handle it, and we might end up clearing through the whole village. I couldn't sit on my ass waiting to cherry-pick a confirmed kill or two while Marc, my subordinate, did the bulk of the work on the mission. I trusted him and needed to let him do what he did so well.

The platoon was working fast, and by the time I caught up to them and made my two-story climb of the compound they were almost ready to move. The residents of the compound confirmed our second stop for the night, a compound on the northern edge of the village. They told us some IMU guys would bunk out there. It corresponded with what our intel told us, and that was good enough. Platoon Sergeant Pack sent Two-Four's squad, a machine-gun team, to check it out.

Despite my elevated position I couldn't see much. I called up Two-Four to let him know I was coming with, knowing the platoon sergeant and platoon leader would hear me. The hardest part of being a Ranger leader, hands down, is keeping track of where all your men are, while the worst thing that can happen is friendly fire. I think we would all rather be overrun and killed together than have to live with the mistake of killing one of our own. I didn't envy the colossal mental effort our leaders had to employ in order to keep track of everyone.

I found some open ground between the compound and the village where I had good fields of view and started scanning. There was an irrigation trench near me I could use for cover, but I stayed on a knee, fairly visible in the moonlight.

"Seven, Sierra-Three," Marc called for the platoon sergeant.

"Go for, Seven," Platoon Sergeant Pack answered back.

"Seven, there's a mass exodus happening. It looks like all the women and children are leaving. They're all heading to the east. BREAK," Marc said, then. "It looks like the whole village, maybe a hundred women and children. There are no MAMs that I can see."

"All right, Sierra-Three, keep eyes on," Platoon Sergeant Pack said. Then he said "BREAK" to keep the net clear. "All 2nd Platoon elements, we know this means an attack is imminent. Squad leaders adjust security. Make sure we don't have any gaps."

I watched the women and children streaming out of the village, maybe one or two hundred of them. I wondered where they'd go. I was thankful they wouldn't be in the cross fire of the battle I knew was coming. This was much different from what I had experienced in the southeastern part of the country. Down south around Kandahar, the Taliban would use women and children as human

Maj Dan helps to calm a child with a chocolate chip granola bar.

(Copyright United States Army)

Maj Dan walking point into our first ambush in Musa Qala.

(Copyright United States Army)

Sergeant Ryan Picou and I pull security while Maj Dan leads an interrogation of villagers meant to draw us into an ambush.

(Copyright United States Army)

Caught in the middle, a group of village elders are compelled to draw us out in the open so foreign fighters can ambush us. We go through the motions and begin a cursory search while we wait to be engaged.

(Copyright United States Army)

Engaging the enemy through a fighting hole during a 180-degree ambush in Musa Qala.

(Copyright United States Army)

I engage enemy fighters during an ambush in Musa Qala.

(Copyright United States Army)

Staff Sergeant Mac pulls overwatch from a ROD site, while we wait for the cover of darkness to move into a hostile village.

(Copyright United States Army)

A Ranger leader takes in the striking beauty of Afghanistan's mountains while monitoring radio communications. *(Copyright United States Army)*

Our heaviest hitting weapons system, a Ranger mortar section, beats back Taliban Ambushers in Musa Qala.

(Copyright United States Army)

DEA intel leads us to several tons of semi-processed hashish, known locally as "sheesha." *(Copyright United States Army)*

A partially successful attempt to destroy several tons of hashish/sheesha.

(Copyright United States Army)

Marc and me after a 13-kilometer running firefight with Uzbek militants.

Weary from a night of village clearing, Rangers prepare to occupy a ROD site where they will repel attacking Taliban all day.

The "big guys," two of 2nd Platoon's team leaders. I took every opportunity to walk point with these Rangers. *(Copyright United States Army)*

I try to unwind and catch some rest in the "castle" we took over as our ROD site after a night of intense fighting.

(Copyright United States Army)

Back on duty after a short rest, the setting sun means we will soon be fighting through the Uzbek militant-held village near our ROD site.

(Copyright United States Army)

Late spring in northern Afghanistan.

(Copyright United States Army)

Alpha Company Medics roasting a turkey for the boys after a long night of fighting. *(Copyright United States Army)*

The rising sun and fast-approaching CH-47s are welcome after a long cold night in Northern Afghanistan. *(Copyright United States Army)*

A view through my spotting scope of the thousand-foot cliffs that rise from the plains of Mazar Sharif.

(Copyright United States Army)

A Ranger machine gunner takes fire commands from his team leader during an attack on our ROD site. *(Copyright United States Army)*

Rooftop Ranger checks mission progress during a night raid outside of Jalalabad. *(Copyright United States Army)*

A cache of RPGs we found in the Tengi Valley, identical to the ones that shot down CH-47 Extortion 17, killing all aboard.

(Copyright United States Army)

A night vision shot of the severe terrain around Tengi Valley. This terrain has been used as a natural defensive barrier for centuries.

(Copyright United States Army)

A long exposure captures Rangers processing potential fighters disguised as Afghan Nomads. *(Copyright United States Army)*

A team leader and I pulling security in the desert outside a Bedouin encampment. *(Copyright United States Army)*

Bedouin encampment and a custom-painted tractor.

A long exposure shows the vibrant color of a Bedouin encampment lighted by green infrared lasers and red headlamps.

A long exposure of outer cordon securing a perimeter around a Bedouin encampment. *(Copyright United States Army)*

Premission checks complete, Team Merrill takes a load off before launching on a night operation. *(Copyright United States Army)*

What I call the "point of no return" Team Merrill loads a CH-47 for night operations. *(Copyright United States Army)*

A 160th SOAR UH-6 provides close air support during a night raid in Afghanistan. *(Copyright United States Army)*

Rangers run to load a National Guard CH-47 after grueling combat operations in Afghanistan. *(Copyright United States Army)*

A night vision shot of a CH-47 after dropping off members of Team Merrill for night operations. *(Copyright United States Army)*

shields or force their women to hide weapons when we were coming for them.

The courtesy of evacuating women and children is probably how the IMU managed to keep the locals from turning on them. I was thankful for this as well, because it meant that anyone left in the village had stayed to fight. That didn't mean we could "free gun" and blast everyone, but we didn't have to extend them the same benefit of the doubt.

I turned my attention to the northern border of the village. There was a breezeway between two adobe buildings. I could see three men standing in a row under the roof of the breezeway. They were probably in their forties, and they were watching the Rangers take down the isolated compound. In front of them was a low wall, just over waist high. The man on the far left kept turning away from us, checking the progress of the exodus of women and children.

I watched the Afghan men, as well as the exodus, while Two-Four and his Rangers quickly but cautiously processed the compound. They quietly scaled the walls, opened the gate to the exterior, and quickly moved through the living quarters. The building had been abandoned in the last 24 hours; it had perishable food and made-up beds, but no one was home. The squad did a cursory search but was careful to avoid booby traps, then determined it was a dry hole.

The squad picked up and moved back to the compound that Platoon Sergeant Pack and the rest of the platoon were still processing. One of the three men I was watching darted into a doorway. I guessed at his path behind the adobe wall, and my guess was confirmed when I saw his silhouette flash past a small window. The two remaining men hadn't spotted me, but they knew that Two-Four and his boys had their backs turned.

I switched my laser to red-visible and flashed it in the faces of the two remaining men to let them know they shouldn't try anything. Most sane humans in Afghanistan shrink and run when you do this, but these men just snapped their attention to me. ROE didn't say you could shoot someone for being defiant, but I wished at that moment that I could.

The man who returned stopped short of the doorway he had disappeared into, warned, it seemed, by a gesture from his compatriots who had remained outside. I watched his body language, and it looked a lot like mine when I was propping up a gun in a corner next to a doorway—something I had done a thousand times and had seen other Rangers do as well. It wasn't enough to enable me to shoot, but it was getting us closer to making a determination.

"Seven, Sierra-Three." It was Marc's tense voice coming across the net in a scratchy whisper. "Can you send me some guys? I have several enemy personnel with small arms moving northwest toward 1st Platoon."

At first I wondered why Marc hadn't simply engaged with the machine-gun team backing him up.

"Sierra-Three, Seven, roger, where are they?" Platoon Sergeant Pack asked.

"Seven, they're exiting Building One-Oh-One, four hundred fifty meters from me, heading toward building Four," Marc called back. That made more sense to me now. If Marc pulled a shot or our machine gunner was a bit off, a single enemy RPG could turn them all into casualties. It wasn't the choice I would have made, but Marc was doing the right thing. They were not decisively engaged, the enemy didn't even know they were there, and he could afford a bit of tactical patience to turn the odds in our favor.

"Roger, Sierra. BREAK. Two-One, get over there and take the AT, don't let them get out of our AO." It was Platoon Sergeant Pack directing a squad to essentially block the seven guys from leaving our Area of Operation and ambushing 1st Platoon.

"AT, good, copy," Sergeant B called back.

"Two-One, good copy," Staff Sergeant Reggie echoed, and they headed out on an intercept path. They would move west of Marc, who would engage the enemy with sniper fire and the machine gun team if they tried to run back the way they came.

They were soon in position, but the six IMU fighters had spotted us and hidden themselves in another outbuilding.

Sergeant B moved into position and got to a knee, putting his RAWS over his soldier like a bazooka. Skinny Pete loaded it with an HEDP (High-Explosive, Dual-Purpose) cartridge. He took aim at the small building and fired. I could hear the 84-mm high-explosive round detonate. Yet it had little effect on the super-strong adobe wall. Sergeant

B would later tell me it just blackened the wall. You wouldn't want to be inside, but we all expected the massively powerful antitank round to defeat the small structure.

"Hit it again, AT," Staff Sergeant John called.

Skinny Pete loaded another round, and Sergeant B fired again, hitting the building dead center. The people inside were rattled, for sure, but unharmed.

Two-One moved up to try to enter the building, but the enemy fighters came out of a door and started spraying them with their AK-47s. The Ranger squad answered with precise three-round bursts.

I could hear the firefight from the other side of the village as its pitch increased to a noise. The battle lasted for only a minute—maybe two at the outside—but it was an eternity for all of us.

The three men I was watching were shifting slightly and passing something back and forth between them at waist level. Whatever it was they were passing was obscured by the wall in front of them. They seemed completely unfazed by the violent battle being waged just a few hundred meters away.

"BREAK, BREAK, BREAK. All elements north of Phase Line Broncos consolidate at Building Twenty," Platoon Sergeant Pack called over the net with deliberate calmness and clarity.

I needed to pick up and go, but before I could move out I saw one of the men I was watching reach into the doorway he had come out of earlier. I lifted Miss America to my shoulder and trained my IR laser on his face. I took the slack out of my two-stage trigger.

The first man's hand came back out with a long bundle, and I eased back the remaining one-and-a-quarter pounds of trigger pressure. Before I could register the hit I shifted my aim, illuminating the second man's face, and pulled all the way through the trigger without pausing. Miss America bucked gently into my shoulder a second time, and I swung my laser beam to the right, onto the third man, who had turned to his compatriots.

I could see the shock on his face as he registered what was happening. *Heads bob and move, bodies don't.* The words of Ed Holmeyer, one of my instructors from the Special Forces Sniper Course, echoed in my head. I lowered my aim across the top of his shoulders, which were now at an oblique angle to me, and squeezed off another round.

He disappeared straight down behind the low wall like a puppet cut from his strings. I paused after my final shot and let Miss America's barrel drop slightly, looking with the wider field of view for any movement from any of the three men.

Suddenly a Kuchi dog came charging toward me, barking and snarling, doing its best impression of a wolf. I trained my laser on the dog and without looking through the scope sent a round lengthwise through the beast. That dropped him, and he rolled onto his back and groaned.

The firefight behind me was dwindling down to pop shots of mostly M4s. I picked up my gear and ran back toward Building 20, getting there in time to fall in with the last of the platoon that was moving south toward the fire-fight.

I linked up with Marc at his blocking position and asked him if he had shot anyone. He shook his head no. I knew he was disappointed.

A couple of our guys went into the building we had hit with the RAWS. They found one EKIA as well as an RPG. Other Rangers checked the EKIA who were right outside the building.

The rest of the enemy the platoon engaged were far away and not visible to us, so we didn't check them to determine how many EKIA there were.

We called for exfil and skirted the northwest edge of the village, then headed due north. We walked across the softly rolling hills that were like rippling water frozen in time. The short green grass reminded me of the tundra grasses on the Montana and Colorado steppes, but the pleasantly cool desert air made me think of an arid green springtime around Bakersfield, California.

7

SIMO SHOT

The fighting season was in full swing, and we continued our missions out of Mazar-i-Sharif. Most were single- or dual-platoon missions, and most of our HVTs were IMU fighters who were thought to be leaders of that movement.

In a perfect world, Team Merrill would have rotated to Afghanistan as one unit, and we'd all be there until we redeployed back to the States as a group. But nothing in this world is perfect, and in war even less so.

Marc and Hank were coming up on the end of their Army contracts, and like the rest of 3rd Ranger Battalion they were close to rotating home, while the rest of us would stay with Alpha Company in Afghanistan for several more months.

Although it's never said, there's something in your DNA as a soldier that while it's tragic to lose a comrade, it's doubly tragic to lose a fellow Ranger who is just a few days or weeks away from going home. This is especially true on a rotation where every mission is a direct action against a determined enemy, and where that direct action is preceded and followed by a death-defying helicopter ride.

Marc, my sniper teammate, was especially on my mind as we settled into our briefing in the TOC. Mac and I had already decided that we'd pull double duty as snipers to keep Marc out of the heat of battle as much as possible. Mac would do most of the dynamic work—climbing compound walls and rooftops—while I'd pull outer security. Our platoon sergeant decided to have Hank either work with the ROD platoon or stay at the FOB. No one thought anything less of these men for being assigned to these less risky positions. It was just the way we operated.

Mac and I had been taking Marc or Hank's place when our missions only called for a single platoon and its two-man sniper team. Despite their "short-time," Marc and Hank weren't happy about it. Mac and I, on the other hand, were firm that we were doing the right thing. You can't control what happens once the gears of war start turning, but you could sometimes buy a little bit of space. It also meant that Mac and I skipped most of our nights off and that we were hunting twice as much. Unlike Marc and Hank, we didn't have an eye to the future; we were already living out our dreams.

We were getting into a regular rhythm here at MES, and in the waning afternoon light we found ourselves in yet another intel briefing. There was a massing of IMU and foreign fighters in the area, and there was at least one HVT with them. Up here in northern Afghanistan, the locals sometimes fed us intelligence when they thought we could get them out from under the IMU's thumb. We had a name and a place, and that made it a point raid. We'd follow that up with the traditional Team Merrill work of clearing through the surrounding village and occupying a ROD site. Mac and I agreed we would do the legwork of clearing the village, and Marc and Hank could pull overwatch for 2nd Platoon, which was tasked with occupying and fortifying our ROD site.

After the briefing in the TOC, our platoon sergeant introduced us to our new camera guy, Jose. If you've ever wondered how those scenes of Americans in combat wind up on the news, more often than not it's because a member of the Combat Camera troop takes them, especially if it's the kind of action Rangers get into, where it's vastly too dangerous to have a civilian media person tag along.

Jose's call sign was "Com Cam"—short for Combat Cameraman—and we were told that he'd be accompanying us on this mission. We learned that he had no combat experience, and that meant we'd have to look out for him. That typically complicated things, because the Com Cam guys always wanted to be in position for the best shot and videos, which was almost always *in* the action. That left it to the rest of us to keep the Com Cam guys from getting their heads blown off while they did their work.

Sometimes it was really tense trying to find the right balance for Com Cam guys, but Jose seemed levelheaded enough to keep from being a liability. He didn't exactly fit the mold of a Ranger, and he wasn't one, but he was a fellow soldier who had volunteered for this dangerous mission, so we wanted to treat him with the dignity and respect he deserved, while at the same time not putting him in harm's way and not putting a Ranger in jeopardy trying to cover his butt. I can say this now because Jose stuck with us for the remainder of our rotation in Afghanistan. While none of us would lay odds during that first meeting that he'd be anything but a liability, he quickly rose to the occasion and turned out to be one hell of a soldier.

For this mission, 2nd Platoon was the first out the door, as their mission was to secure our ROD site. We learned later that their infil was complicated by the fact that their Chinooks landed in a walled-in field. There was no gate and no way out except over the walls. This actually wasn't that uncommon. Afghanistan is a rocky country, and farmers used those rocks with their ubiquitous adobe to cordon off their fields. My Ranger buddies who are from New England tell me it's a lot like where they're from.

Second Platoon's infil route was complicated even more because some fields in that area had been intentionally flooded, and many seemed like they were built in such a way as to hold the rainwater. Since spring is the rainy season, it seemed like every farmer had his own lake. While Rangers are pretty adept at humping our own gear, even our heavy machine guns, over long distances, the heaviest stuff that we take on some infils are our Speedballs. Believe me, once we got to the ROD site, we heard from 2nd Platoon about how they had to commandeer donkeys from the compound and, using the heavy ropes we carry on all our missions, haul those Speedballs over walls and drag them to the ROD site.

Once 2nd Platoon was out the door, 1st Platoon mustered on at the MES airfield and we waited for our Chinooks. There was something about being with 1st Platoon again that put me at ease. Mac and I had deployed with them the year before, and we'd done some successful joint Ranger-SEAL operations near Jalalabad, in Nangarhar Province in eastern Afghanistan.

I mentioned before that after flying only with the 160th SOAR on our missions out of Kandahar in southern Afghanistan, we were initially skeptical when National Guard helos showed up to lift us to an op. But it didn't take us long to learn that these National Guard aircrew were as professional as any of us in the "regular" Army—and boy, could they handle those birds.

During the short flight to our objective area, Mac and I went over our procedures and made sure we had planned for the unexpected—and there was always the unexpected. We landed about 6 klicks from our target compound and made a fast march to get into position before anyone was alerted to our presence.

We managed to get there without stirring up any hostiles along the route. So far, so good. We set up a cordon around the compound, and the assault team surreptitiously entered. Then, as he had done many times before, Zeke got on the bullhorn and began calling the residents out of the building. Soon the assault Rangers were separating the residents and questioning them. Most military-age males got zip cuffs and continued to be questioned.

That done, the platoon searched the living quarters and outbuildings. These structures were inside the walls of the compound and were the same kind of outbuildings you'd find on a big farm: several stalls for livestock, an overhang for agricultural equipment, and the motos that are everywhere in Afghanistan.

I mention all this only because we'd learned the hard way that just because a structure was, say, a chicken coop, it could still provide effective cover for an enemy bent on ambushing us from behind. But the worst case would be that it was being used as a homemade explosive lab because, like a meth lab, those things had a tendency to blow up unexpectedly. We'd paid the price in blood for not clearing every building that could hide a human, and we didn't want to pay that price again.

Meanwhile, Mac slipped inside the compound and climbed up on a number of rooftops until he found the one with the best vantage point—one with a clear view of the main road through the village we'd need to walk through to get to our next target village. While Mac was doing that, I walked around the compound looking for anywhere where we might have a gap in security.

From my vantage point, it seemed pretty quiet. My sense of ease made me think of the phrase "calm before the storm." This area was loaded with IMU, we had been hitting them hard for the last few weeks, and it was all but inevitable they would come out and fight us toe-to-toe.

I knew Mac had a good view and field of fire to the north, east, and south, so I found a bit of high ground about 25 meters from the compound that gave me a good vantage point looking north, northwest, and west. This may sound like a simple thing, but at night, after you've fast-marched a half-dozen klicks, with intel telling you the enemy was massing in this area, and with the assault team already zip-tying bad guys, we had to tamp down the adrenaline and ensure we were covering our other Rangers as best as we possibly could. That's what overwatch is all about.

I listened to the 1st Platoon squad leaders making calls to Major Kearney as they searched and cleared all the buildings and structures in the compound. Based on the radio chatter, it appeared that all the MAMs who were questioned were just villagers and not IMU. I was disappointed to say the least: we were supposed to be tracking down a "massed" IMU enemy.

We had an AC-130 Spectre gunship overhead, and the radios came alive as the aircrew reported seeing two men leave a nearby village and begin picking their way toward us. The Spectre crew couldn't tell for certain if the men were armed, but they were worried nonetheless, and so were we. It had been too damned quiet for too long, and this smelled like an ambush.

The radio crackled again. "Sierra, One-Seven, see if you can get eyes on." It was Platoon Sergeant Will calling Mac. The call from the Spectre gunship had him worried. "Spectre says they came from somewhere around building four," Wes continued. As we planned our missions, we always gave buildings numbers just so we could talk tactically with some accuracy. We'd learned the hard way that being imprecise with terms like "That building by the fork in the road" or "That two-story building over by the outbuildings" was a surefire way to get our own guys killed or to shoot an innocent civilian. So while creating a numbering scheme like this originally struck me as a little anal, it helped to keep us alive, so we went with it.

"Roger, Seven," Mac replied. Then I heard his transmission cut out with a click. "Sierra-One," Mac began again. "Start cheating north and see if you can catch them when they get to the open ground."

"Roger," I called back.

I got up, crossed the small road north of the compound, and began scanning. Soon I saw movement.

"Sierra-One has eyes on. No PID, but they're maneuvering," I said. "Maneuvering" meant they were moving in the way a fighter would, keeping low, sticking to the shadows, and just generally being sneaky and suspicious. I could just make out their shapes as they crept away from the village and made their way west.

"Roger, Sierra," Seven called back to Mac and me. "Spectre says they have eyes on possible weapons. These guys are heading to the wadi."

That wasn't good news. It meant these guys were using the terrain as good cover. Invisible to us in the low ground was a dried-up riverbed, or "wadi." These wadis were always littered with boulders, old river rocks, and sand, yet the Afghans moved down them with surprising ease and speed. It was a high-speed getaway route for them, but for us, with our heavy kit, these wadis were an impediment. Trying to dash through one with a hundred pounds of gear in the dark of night was a good way to break an ankle—or worse. We'd learned that the hard way on many previous ops.

There was silence over the net for a few seconds, while Platoon Sergeant Wes and the 1st Platoon's leader discussed what to do next. After talking it over with Major Dan, they decided to send 3rd Squad—One-Three—along with a machine-gun team and Major Dan's element (our JTAC, call sign Stryker, and our Com Cam guy, Jose) and Mac and me to do "squirter chase." That means any MAMs—armed or not—who try to flee an objective area.

We knew we needed to get these squirters for a number of reasons—not least because they could alert other IMU fighters in the area and we could be quickly outnumbered and overwhelmed. We got a quick count of the men in each element of our group. Mac climbed down from his rooftop vantage point, linked up with me, and we moved north about 100 meters, where we had a good view of the wadi.

Suddenly, the two men in the wadi started sprinting. Something must have alerted them to our presence, and they were trying to get out any way they could. We were trying to close the distance, but we were slogging through muddy furrowed fields, half running and half falling.

Meanwhile, these guys were using their familiarity with the wadi to put distance between them and us. We were quickly reminded that this was an away game.

"Up in the back," one of 3rd Squad's team leaders called over the net, meaning we had all personnel accounted for and could turn on the speed.

Mac and I were running all out. I could hear Mac breathing heavily as we paused to shoulder our rifles. We could see much farther than the line guys and were hoping for a shot at the two men that would save our boys some running.

All we caught was a glimpse of motion twisting through the wadi, obscured by sparse trees.

"Up here, Balls. There's a bit of a goat path," Mac said, indicating the higher solid ground between the wadi and the village.

He nodded in the direction. I saw the path and simply replied, "Roger."

It wasn't much of a path, but it gave us a good angle from which to shoot at the fleeing men and not hit our chase team, which was off to our left. We picked our way through the wadi, running as fast as we could while we paralleled our chase team in the riverbed. We would pause and quickly scan the west bank of the wadi to try for a clear shot at the squirters. The twisting wadi and rolling terrain didn't give us many options.

As we kept pace with the fleeing men and our own chase team, we had to jump a few walls and dip down into the wadi when our route was impassable. We were just behind, or even with, our chase team as they doggedly fought their way through the rocky riverbed.

I watched the chase team try to keep up with the squirters as first one, then another Ranger would falter and go down, cracking hard on a knee, only to spring back up without a second's hesitation. In sports they say sacrifice the body. The 1st Platoon's chase team was exemplifying that, and the rocky wadi terrain was taking its toll. I knew how painful those falls were, and even the ample adrenaline we had coursing through our veins didn't lessen that shock. Yet there was no hesitation on their part. They simply wouldn't be stopped or even slowed.

Finally, the terrain opened up and we could see the running men clearly zigzagging toward some wooded hilly terrain. Mac didn't quite have a shot, but I thought I might. I stopped and blew out hard to clear my lungs, doing everything I could to force my body to calm down.

I saw a team leader, Sergeant Abeyta, directly in front of me, almost in line with the fleeing squirter. I shouldered Miss America and saw that they both were in my scope. No good. Just then, Sergeant Abeyta slid to a stop to shoulder *his* rifle.

I could see the fleeing man over his right shoulder and took aim, remembering that I had subsonic rounds and needed to hold high to reach the man, who was only about 100 meters from me. I counted two-and-one-half tic marks in my reticle, centered that point between the fleeing man's shoulders, and fired.

Sergeant Abeyta's round was an echo of mine, but

something was wrong. My gun failed to cycle because of the much quieter, weaker subsonic round. *Damnit, damnit, damnit,* I cursed to myself.

"Malfunction!" I hissed to Mac, who was just shouldering his rifle, instinctively picking up my slack.

At the same moment I heard five steady pops from Sergeant Abeyta's weapon, followed by a louder noise of pops as the rest of his squad zeroed in on the squirters and cut them to ribbons.

I locked back my bolt, ripped out my mag, and replaced it with a new one. I smacked the side of my rifle hard, tripping the bolt release that forcefully chambered a fresh sonic round with a satisfying "chunk" sound.

"Gun up," I half shouted to Mac, letting him know I was back in the fight.

I took a knee to steady myself, but by then the rifle squad had made it to the first bit of high ground and was kicking the enemy's weapons away and searching the bodies.

"Look left," Mac ordered. He'd already shifted back into overwatch mode while the line Rangers converged on the bodies of the two squirters to confirm that they were dead. They also needed to grab their AK-47s to support the inevitable after-action report and prove we had shot armed MAMs.

"Roger, light on, nine o'clock, two-story compound," I replied. We were both looking at a large compound about 300 meters away that had suddenly come to life.

"I see movement, silhouettes on the balcony, no guns," Mac called back. "Keep scanning."

"I've got left," I replied. Even without Mac telling me where he was looking, I knew he would scan right.

"Balls, ten o'clock, look here!" Mac began urgently, indicating the spot with his IR laser. "Two guys, looks like they're carrying rifles."

I shifted to the direction he was shining his laser on and looked through my scope. One man disappeared into a seam between two mounds of earth, but the other, who was clearly carrying an AK-47, remained in view and was heading straight for 3rd Squad.

"Roger, Mac, PID weapon," I replied as I found the enemy with my scope. The man was covering ground fast and heading up a small hill.

"Two hundred meters," Mac said. It was half-statement, half-question.

"One seventy-five," I replied evenly, as I kept the target in my sights.

"Roger," Mac said calmly. We both were controlling our breathing cycle instinctively, one breath, then two.

We fired simultaneously, and our guns coughed through their suppressors and made a single sound.

The fleeing man's right arm flailed up as his bottom half crumpled. Mac had caught him high, likely blasting a clavicle into his lung. My round had struck low, hitting his spine or shattering his pelvis. His momentum and the shock of bullets hitting bone rolled him over the crown of the hill.

"Hit!" Mac called.

"Hit," I replied.

I heard Mac's SR-25 cough again and I ticked off another round. We could see a bit of humped clothing and a flailing limb barely peaking over the hill. The hump disappeared, but we could still see something flailing, so Mac and I continued to take careful aim and continued to loop rounds at the man, skimming the top of the berm hoping to hit him with the falling trajectory of our bullets.

"Sierra, what are you shooting at?" It was Major Dan's distinct voice on the net.

"We PIDed two personnel with AK's. We engaged one, he's fixed, but he's moving," Mac said.

"Roger, Sierra, stand by," Major Dan ordered. He then continued, "We're rolling in the gunship."

"Sierra, Stryker, fire mission inbound, confirm location of enemy personnel."

"You've got him, Stryker," Mac said.

Damn, those Spectres are the best! I thought. It was like the light of some terrible god shining down before he let loose his lightning bolts.

A minute later we heard the hollow *thunk, thunk, thunk, thunk* of 40-mm rounds as they spit out of the gunship. The rounds crashed into the earth with four corresponding explosions, blowing dirt and white-hot shrapnel into the air.

Our JTAC reengaged with the AC-130, and we heard four more thunks and watched again for the corresponding explosions on the ground.

"Sierra, Stryker, confirm effects on target," our JTAC ordered.

"Good shot, target destroyed," Mac replied. With that confirmation, 3rd Squad moved deliberately toward the area that was now churned-up earth.

I pulled out a handheld thermal scope from a pouch and scanned the area around them, searching for the other man, the one we lost between the berms. Meanwhile, Mac was talking with 3rd Squad's leader, describing the exact area where we had last seen the second man.

They found him—well, most of him—half buried in the fresh dirt tilled up by the explosives. His gun was nowhere to be found.

"Sierra, you sure he had a weapon?" Major Dan called over the net. "Our boys can't find a weapon."

Mac put his hand on the transmit button of his mic and looked at me before pressing it.

"You saw his gun, right?" Mac asked.

"He had an AK in his right hand, and he was carrying it at his waist," I replied.

"You're sure?" Mac asked again. He didn't doubt that he had seen it, but if they didn't find a weapon we would be investigated. And since he was team leader, the bulk of the blame for shooting an unarmed man would fall on his shoulders.

Two of our sniper buddies, working for another task force, had just been through a rigorous investigation for killing the HVT who was the subject of a kill mission. That's something that was unique to our situation. We could do real jail time if we make a mistake and take a life without justification.

"I'm positive, Mac," I replied. "Those rounds buried half of a man. That AK could be buried three feet deep for all we know," I continued, remembering my last sight of the man, AK in one hand, the other flailing over his head as our rounds cut through him.

"Damn, that's right!" Mac replied. I could hear the relief in his voice. The 40-mm rounds from Spectre packed a big punch, and they could simultaneously blow you up and bury you under a meter of earth.

Mac keyed his mic. "Roger, sir. Sierra-One and I confirm PID. The 40-mm rounds likely buried his AK."

There was a long silence before Major Dan replied, "Roger."

Mac dialed his radio to the command frequency Major Dan used to communicate with our JTAC, listened in, and then told me they were discussing that likelihood.

After another long silence, Stryker confirmed that, based on the volume of fire the AC-130 had poured out, the AK could be completely buried, or blown to bits and then buried.

We completed our BDA (battle damage assessment) and called up the number of EKIA and weapons we found. After that, we all regrouped, and 1st and 2nd Platoon met back at Building 4. No one we questioned could provide any additional information about the men we killed.

As we always did, we told the villagers to tell the Taliban and the IMU to come kill us, and we passed out some of the same leaflets we'd distributed in other villages. Then we headed for the ROD site to hunker down for our next mission the following night.

When we dragged ourselves into the compound, we saw an amazing sight. There was Sergeant Reggie, our muscle-bound mascot, dressed in his full kit on a white donkey. "Welcome to your castle," he said with a toothy grin. It was jarring and bizarre.

Our little sniper group—Mac, Marc, Hank, and me— quartered together at the ROD site. When you know you're going to fight together, you try to do everything together.

Exhausted or not, the first thing a Ranger does after a firefight is get his kit and weapons ready for the next fight. Once I was inside the compound the first thing I did was look for the Speedball so I could replace my empty mags with full ones. My replacements were made of polymer, and dragging them to the compound had ground them down to where they were useless. I simply emptied them and re-filled my depleted steel magazines. It did mean I only had my standard load out, just enough to get through a night of fighting. I couldn't load down with several hundred rounds for the day's fighting, as I usually did in our ROD sites.

Once we got our kit and ammo squared away, our platoon sergeant gathered us around and said simply, "Time for breakfast, men."

Platoon Sergeant Pack made a small wood fire and we scavenged potatoes, rice, and eggs from the living quarters of the compound. Doc, our medic, killed a chicken, and we boiled that with the rice. Then we cracked a few fresh eggs and stirred them into our soup. We added a butter packet and a seasoning packet from an MRE. The eggs were so fresh, they tasted amazing. We must have killed a laying hen, though, because that chicken was as tough as beef jerky. All in all, when you're in the fight living on MREs, having a breakfast like this made us all feel we were human beings again, and it was a much appreciated luxury.

I was super-exhausted, but I knew what I needed to do next was find a good sniper hide. I climbed up to the second story of the main house, where I had a good vantage point of the surrounding area. There was a room with a small balcony, just right for a good sniper hide.

Corporal Tog, a team leader, was up there already, and he'd set up a machine gun nest. I've already said what a deadly combination a sniper and a machine-gun team make. After setting up my gear and Miss America, I bedded down and got some rack in that cold adobe room. There is a certain comfort you get from sleeping next to a heavy machine gun manned by battle-hardened Rangers, and sleep found me quickly.

I woke up around 1500 feeling more well-rested than I had in a long time. Corporal Tog, his ammo bearer, and I discussed our tactics. I wasn't very hungry, but I choked down as much of an MRE as I could. I knew I might not get another chance to eat before we got back to MES, and that was a long way off, even if things went according to plan. One of the most stressful things about these missions is that we never knew exactly when we'd exfil. It might be that afternoon, or that night, or dawn the next day. The point is, you had to be ready whenever.

My meal over, I made my way out onto the balcony and took out my small laminated map of the area. I had committed much of the area to memory before sacking out earlier in the day, and I went back over what I could remember, remeasuring distances and directions and going over the numbers we had assigned to the buildings in the village.

I looked at each building through my scope and checked out each window and door. I could see curtains blowing in some of the windows, and I could see people moving past them. They could be families going about their lives or IMU fighters making preparations and waiting for their moment to strike—there was just no way to tell. I noted which buildings were occupied and then catalogued them from closest to farthest. I tried to match the roads and footpaths I could see on the overhead map with what I saw on the ground. Our enemies would inevitably have to use those passages, and I ranged the parts of them that I could see, as well as the buildings. It was a total team effort, because armed with this information, especially what buildings and roads had the most traffic, Corporal Tog and I were on precisely the same page. Now we had to do the hardest thing in combat—wait.

While we waited, a couple of the guys were taking "cool guy pictures." I'd be lying if I said I didn't share their sense of ease. We had lived in dozens of ROD sites, and the near-impenetrable adobe walls were a comforting contrast to the skin-prickling feeling you had when you walked into a Taliban- or IMU-controlled village in the dead of night. The soft afternoon light, the crisp spring air coming from the massive snowcapped mountains, and the pink of blooming fruit trees all added to our feeling of ease.

It was exciting to be living out of a pouch on my back, my only possessions my gun and my kit, with my Ranger buddies and the vague sense of something "back home" that mattered less and less with each mission.

I posed for a picture and couldn't contain a smile. I felt like whatever was back home was worth never seeing again to be right here, right now. With those snowcapped peaks on the horizon, Miss America in my hand, and my Ranger brothers next to me, everything made sense. My existence was distilled down to the barest of things, and I felt the clarity of being completely in the moment.

Corporal Tog's ammo bearer, a private on his first deployment, snapped a couple of quick pictures of me doing my "tough guy" pose. We looked at the digital display together and he said with a laugh, "That one there will get you laid, Sergeant."

I smiled, but before I could join his chuckle, a sharp whoosh-crack shattered the moment. That was immediately followed by another, deeper cracking sound.

We hit the dirt, and my ears pricked with the whistle of another incoming mortar round. I placed the mortar location to the south. It had impacted Building 1, a shack made mostly of rubble and sticks that Two-Two had occupied. The shack was a short distance from the big, solid walls of the compound and was our weakest point. My first thought was, *I hope Marc wasn't on that roof made of sticks.*

Another *whoosh-crack* shattered my thoughts. Then there were more whistling mortar rounds followed by two booming explosions to our west. 1st Platoon was getting hammered, too. The net erupted with calls conveying distance and direction of the enemy fire. Platoon Sergeant Pack called asking for casualty reports. Thus far, thankfully, there were none.

Automatic fire from the north battered my position. Corporal Tog laid on the trigger of his M240 machine gun, burning through two or three hundred rounds in an instant, hammering away at the muzzle flashes. I heard the other 240s and SAWs doing the same, firing in every direction, pouring Ranger machine-gun fire at the enemy's positions. The sound was a roar, and as we poured out more and more fire, it reached a deafening roar.

We were like a lion on a train track bellowing at a freight train that was barreling toward us. It was as if our collective rage, expressed as violence, could stop death itself from plowing through us and scattering us to the wind. I could feel the blood behind my eyes and the throbbing in my neck and temples. There was no controlled breathing. I just jammed myself against a wall and leveled Miss America at the nearest compound. Flashes and silhouettes were all the details I could make out in the windows and doors.

I ignored the mortars raining down on us. If one of them had my number on it, there was nothing I could do. I fired in a triangular pattern at each silhouette, just as my old sniper partner, Stuart, had taught me when we were going through the Special Forces Sniper Course. In moments like this your training comes back to you, even the exact words and actual voices of your instructors from years ago. *Left to right, bottom to top, search in a pattern.* Their lessons were a tonic that quenched the rising feeling of panic I felt.

I fired at a silhouette and saw a flash of a dishdash fall at an odd angle. I moved to the next window and fired at a flashing muzzle, and the movement stopped. *Shoot what you can see*, Mac had often told me when we drilled together. I moved my sniper scope to the next window, but there was nothing to see. I sent several rounds through the window, making sure to hit the left and right edges of the window frame. If anyone was hiding there, some high-speed dirt in their face would make them think twice about engaging us. Another instructor's admonition came into my brain: *One shot, one kill is for police snipers and the movies. Put lead in the bad guys; your platoon can do the rest.*

I moved on to the next window where I'd seen muzzle flashes. The straight line of the window frame had a bulge, and I fired at that until it fell, taking a fabric curtain down with it. Meanwhile, Tog's gun was hammering out nine-round bursts. I dropped my empty magazine and replaced it with a fresh twenty-rounder. The enemy's fire waned slightly from a constant barrage to a steady but scattered stream of small-arms fire.

Our Ranger Death Blossom had broken the ranks of IMU fighters, separating them from each other and pin-ning them in their fighting positions. Overhead, Kiowas worked with our mortar teams to silence the IMU's heavy weapons. Automatic fire was still pouring in on us, but it was lessening. I moved my sniper scope to the next building and went to work. Tog's bursts followed the impact of my rounds, hammering everything he noticed me shooting at with six- to nine-round bursts. We worked together without a word. Nothing could hide from my scope, and nothing could withstand his heavy machine-gun's barrage.

I saw a foot peek out from a wall 300 meters away. I fired three rounds, and then Tog battered the area with a nine-round burst. If I saw a shadow on a visible bit of road I fired three rounds, and Tog would follow it up with a blast from his M240. I changed magazines again, shifted my aim west as far as I could see, and took aim at a more distant group of buildings. I scanned, saw muzzle flashes, and sent rounds after them while bullets snapped over my head. Tog's machine gun was pummeling an irrigation trench in the dead center of our sector of fire, and the Rangers next to me peppered the area with their M4's and 40-mm grenades.

Two-One and Two-Four made their way to the rooftop and we volleyed back and forth with our enemy, bursts of fire coming at us every other second. Our machine guns swiveled across their sectors, pausing to send suppressing fire where they saw or suspected movement.

Suddenly I felt something burst to the right of me, and a shock of pain jarred my head. I ducked to a knee behind the wall and raised my right hand to my ear. Two-One looked at me with alarm. I realized his muzzle brake was right next to my ear. I couldn't help giving him a dirty look. He could have ruptured my eardrum or burned my face.

"Shit! Are you okay, man?" he asked. He looked like he'd just run over his dog.

"I'm good, man!" I replied with a genuine smile. I was elated that I wasn't actually injured.

After a brief chuckle, we turned our attention back to the enemy. The fighting nearest to us was dying down, but we were still getting sporadic fire from all sides every few minutes. We were trying to pinpoint the last of the IMU fighters and answer their irregular fire. I still found shadows to shoot at, but the muzzle flashes I saw were 700 meters or more away and were obscured by brush. These weren't exactly good shots, and I was burning through ammo too damn fast.

"Watch and shoot! Watch and shoot!" Two-One and Two-Four echoed each other, and the rest of us shouted the command back, both to them and to each other.

There was a lull in the fighting for a few minutes, with just some scattered fire from the enemy's Soviet-era weapons. Everything on the ground was different from what we had seen on the overhead images, and we were trying to pin down which buildings were which and direct our fire at the buildings where we still saw muzzle flashes.

Suddenly there was another wave of enemy automatic fire from all directions. It was nothing like their initial barrage but was still intense. The enemy had regrouped, and tactically this was almost as impressive as their coordinated initial barrage. They gave us everything they had with a textbook infantry-style attack. It was exactly how we would have attacked if our roles had been reversed. I had to give grudging respect to the IMU. We had bitten a huge chunk out of their forces, but they still wanted more.

Our machine guns answered the enemy fire, and the rest of us searched the places we had found them before.

"It's poppin' off! That's us, baby!" Sergeant Reggie shouted, as if the enemy could hear him and his verbal barrage were as deadly as the 40-mm grenades he was lobbing at them.

"Sierra, you see where that's coming from?" Reggie asked.

"Twelve o'clock, four fifty, maybe five hundred," I replied, measuring the distance in meters as accurately as I could.

Sergeant Reggie started launching 40-mm grenades, aiming at where I indicated. It was the maximum range for our grenade launchers, but it had the right effect and got the enemy moving. That brought them under our guns again, and we began to pick them off.

Those of us with a few deployments under our belt had spent plenty of time chasing ghostlike fighters, often with nothing concrete to show for it. Now, even though we were getting hammered with intense enemy fire, we were grateful that the enemy had decided to stand and fight. The sun was setting quickly, and every minute brought us closer to coming out of our walls and running these guys down like dogs.

One of Two-One's privates disappeared down a ladder and soon reappeared with bandoliers of 40-mm grenades and belts of machine-gun ammo.

"Sierra, where is that machine-gun fire coming from?" Two-Four shouted.

"Behind that wood line, at eleven o'clock, there is a satellite dish at nine hundred meters," I replied.

"What satellite dish?" Two-Four asked dubiously. There aren't many satellite dishes in northern Afghanistan, but if it looked like one to me, I figured it would look like one to him when he saw it.

"The wood line is five or six hundred meters away. *Behind* that satellite dish and *beneath* that, you can see the flash," I replied emphatically.

I knew I couldn't snake a bullet through all that scrubby brush, especially at that range. But that's why I love a machine gun. Miss America is a scalpel. Tog's M240 machine gun was a buzz saw that could tear through the trees and brush with ease.

"Roger, walk me on to them," Two-Four ordered.

"Roger, eyes on," I replied as I focused my scope on the faintly blinking light. Two-Four gave Corporal Tog a rough area to fire at, and I watched his tracer fly harmlessly away into the distance.

"Right, Five-Zero!" I shouted over the sound of M4s and incoming fire. Corporal Tog had to rely on his experience at that range to know what 50 meters looked like.

"Right, Five-Zero," Two-Four echoed into the machine-gun nest. Corporal Tog's M240 gun ripped off another long burst, and it looked like it went right into the satellite dish. He'd made a perfect correction on the fly.

"Drop, Two-Five," I said deliberately, and Two-Four echoed the command to the machine-gun nest. The tracers arced out and sliced through the thin forest between us and the enemy machine gun, dead on target.

"He's on!" I shouted, and Two-Four relayed the command to Tog. Three long, satisfying bursts arced over the ground and punched through the trees, and that's the last we saw of that IMU machine gunner.

"We have birds inbound for a fire mission, stand by to lift fire." It was our captain's voice over the net, letting us know we had a fire mission working.

A pair of Kiowas appeared on the horizon. The waning enemy fire dried up completely, and the enemy went to ground. They were brave enough to attack and re-attack our ROD site, but they weren't stupid. They knew from experience that attacking us beneath our Kiowas was certain death.

The Kiowas made endless circles over the enemy positions but didn't pour out any of their deadly fire. The enemy had melted away. We remained ready for another wave of attacks, but they never came. We had literally beaten over one hundred IMU into submission.

As night fell, we rebundled our Speedballs, packed up all our gear, and got ready to exfil. When it was fully dark we walked out to our HLZ and waited for our Chinooks. It was the right time to exfil. We were black on 40-mm grenades and really low on M240 ammo, and Mac and I were almost black on sniper ammo. ("Black" is military slang for saying a resource is gone.) I recall leaving there with only fifty rounds or so. Besides fighting for essentially 24 hours straight, I had slimmed down my kit over the last few missions so that now I was only carrying Miss America, a tomahawk, and one hand grenade.

The flight back to MES was uneventful and we went through our usual routine—debrief, chow, get our weapons and kit back into fighting order, and then blessed rack time.

I probably slept for 12 hours. As soon as my eyes opened I could hear and see the buzz in our tent. We'd gotten a WARNO. We were picking up and moving to Jalalabad, in Nangarhar Province, in eastern Afghanistan. I had been there during my first deployment and again in 2010, during the bloodiest year of the Afghan war. It was Taliban Hillfighter country, and I'd learned the hard way that they were always up for a fight.

8
TANGI VALLEY

Once we got the warning order that we'd be moving on from Mazar-i-Sharif, our morale surged. MES is a well-appointed base, with a café, spacious chow halls, and good gyms. Hell, they even had cobblestone drainage and paved roads. We didn't get to appreciate that much, since our unexpected arrival meant they had to scrape the bottom of the barrel for our billeting. We were tired of living on top of each other, packed into tents like sardines, living out of our rucks, and packing up and moving every few weeks.

On the other hand, we knew we wouldn't be in JBAD for very long—a couple weeks at most. But there was a sunk cost in understanding the local geography, topography, weather, demographics, and especially the enemy. In the last case, I can't say I ever figured out our enemy in Afghanistan. Trying to get your brain around the amorphous groups of men who murder their fellow citizens and terrorize the ones they don't kill, all while claiming a religious moral prerogative. is something our entire Ranger Regiment struggled with, and something I struggle with to this day.

Once our platoon sergeants told us we were picking up and deploying to Jalalabad we became intel hounds. We spent a lot of time in the TOC, scrounging up whatever intel we could on what the enemy was doing in and around Jalalabad. Several of our fellow Rangers had operated out of JBAD during previous rotations, so we pumped them for information.

For most of us, it wasn't a surprise we were rotating to JBAD. It is the second-largest city in eastern Afghanistan, right behind the capital of Kabul, which is about 150 klicks to the west. Jalalabad is an ancient city located at the junction of the Kabul River and the Kunar River, near the Laghman valley. It is the capital of Nangarhar Province, as well as the center of social and business activity in the region, because it is close to the Pakistani border. And since Pakistan is the main source of products for all of Afghanistan, Jalalabad is one of the leading trading centers with Pakistan, which meant that there was a constant flow of traffic from Pakistan to Afghanistan, and lots of it went straight through JBAD.

What all that meant to us was that JBAD was only 50 klicks from the Pakistani border, and the worst part of that border, the Federally Administered Tribal Areas. If there is one place in the world where there is no rule of law, it was these areas. I know I'm not being politically correct saying this, but Pakistan had basically given up trying to govern these areas, and it seemed they let the Pakistan Taliban run a country within a country.

No one knows for certain how many Taliban are in the Federally Administered Tribal Areas, but the numbers are surely in the tens of thousands. So we knew going in that if things got hot in JBAD, we'd be facing a potentially un-limited flow of Taliban coming across the border. Our pucker factor was pretty high as we anticipated our move.

Just before leaving MES we had some more personnel rotations. To be completely honest, it was probably the worst possible time to have seasoned and blooded veterans leave us. No matter how well qualified their replacements, the new guys would have to be blended into the team. That was always a challenge, but especially now that we knew we'd be going to JBAD and face the Taliban again.

Marc and Hank were two of the guys who were leav-ing. Both of them had done their duty—and more—and the good-byes and good-lucks brought a lump to our throats.

Marc's replacement was Chris, a sniper team leader himself. He had volunteered to be my subordinate for the latter half of Team Merrill for one reason: he wanted to hunt down and kill Taliban. Chris and I were buddies from Ranger School and had remained friends since then. We had often ridden Harleys together or met up for a Friday-night grill and bull session back at Fort Benning. Most people could walk right past Chris and never guess he was a Ranger. He was slightly built and skinny—so skinny that one of our Ranger School instructors tried to stick him with the nickname P.O.W. He had a shock of black hair and a perpetual five-o'clock shadow.

Chris had a reputation in the sniper community of being a crack shot. Beyond that, he was uber-professional, quiet, funny, and, despite his slight frame, strong as an ox. He wasn't the kind of guy you wanted to race during a run, and he would embarrass most Rangers if you tried to beat him up a mountain.

Hank's replacement was another one of my Ranger School buddies, Wade. He was the polar opposite of Chris. Wade was a big, heavy guy—over 6 feet tall and around 220 pounds. He was also brash, outgoing, and hot-tempered. He sometimes rubbed people the wrong way, but there was something about his quick wit and easy laugh—especially when he was laughing at himself—that took the edge off his abrasive personality. He was a lot like a big, loyal dog who kept annoying you but who you loved anyway.

Wade came in to be Mac's sniper partner. They'd known each other for a long time, served together in the same platoon before they were snipers, and had one of those brotherly love-hate relationships. If you walked by the two of them when they were jawing at each other, you'd swear they were about to get into a fistfight, but they never did. Mac easily tabled any differences he had with Wade for good reason: he was a great sniper and absolutely fearless in a firefight.

We were rousted out in the pre-dawn hours and packed our kit and our weapons aboard C-130 Herks for the 400-klick flight to JBAD. We hadn't gotten any intel on what our missions might be, but as always, we hoped for the best and planned for the worst.

What we saw when we arrived at the U.S. military base outside JBAD revealed a great deal. JBAD was the main base facing the Taliban and other militants who enjoyed safe haven in Pakistan, and it looked the part. To say it was austere would be a huge understatement. The base looked like it was ready to withstand a Taliban attack at any moment, and security was incredibly high.

While it was pretty basic, JBAD was humming. There were a wide variety of military and OGA (other government agencies) based there. We were pretty sure—or at least we hoped—that someone well up the chain of command was coordinating all their efforts, but it certainly seemed as if each of these outfits was just doing its own thing.

MARSOC (Marine Corps Special Operations) guys flew drones out of JBAD to gather intelligence about the local area. We never read into exactly what they were doing, but we figured it was basic reconnaissance. Army Special Forces also flew small drones that were designed to develop intelligence on possible HVTs in the area. We would go on direct action raids to take down some of the HVTs their drones located.

There was also a SEAL team working out of JBAD. We had a long tradition of working with the Navy's special operators. The SEALs are a pretty small organization to begin with, they had a global mission to man, and they were deployed everywhere in the Afghan theater. All that meant they often didn't have the numbers to go on direct action missions by themselves.

Since Rangers are all about direct action, we teamed up with SEALs frequently. We didn't mind taking a supporting role if it meant we were getting to do work. Once we got to JBAD, they were the first guys we linked up with immediately after linking up with the Rangers who were already there. Having access to the highest levels of Navy intel apparatus was a windfall, and the odds that we'd be working together were high.

We were barely settled in to JBAD when we got an intel dump revealing the location of a one-legged IED maker we were calling "Old Joe." Evidently this guy was pretty infamous around JBAD. He'd been doing this a long time—back when he had two legs.

We did a classic night raid, rolling in on a location where he was thought to be, but it turned out to be a dry hole. We regrouped, pored over the intel, and launched again, this time with high confidence that we would catch him. We missed him again, though we did find another man with one leg. Old Joe was a throwback from the Mujahedeen days for a reason; he was as cunning as they came. Back at JBAD, we got some updated intel that was of higher confidence than what we'd had before. A drone tracked him as he rode his motorcycle along an MSR and ultimately to the outskirts of a midsize village.

Working off the drone feed, we launched a Ranger kill squad that tracked him down. As the Rangers closed in on him, an AH-64 Apache Longbow took him down. The Rangers on the ground converged on him a minute later and confirmed he was dead. They also "liberated" his prosthetic leg and brought it to our Company building back at Fort Benning. This may sound a little gruesome, but all three times I'd been to JBAD since 2006 we'd been hunting for this one-legged IED maker, so a trophy seemed appropriate.

These missions were necessary, but we felt like we were nibbling around the edges of really taking a bite out of the Taliban. This sure didn't seem like the reason we packed out of MES in a hurry to come here. That's why it was welcome news when Major Dan and our other leaders told us we'd be mounting up and deploying to Forward Operating Base Shank, about 60 klicks west-southwest of JBAD. The FOB was about a dozen klicks southeast of the city of Baraki Barak, in high desert steppe. It reminded me of the western slope of Colorado—high, dry, and with big mountains on the horizon.

As Forward Operating Bases go, FOB Shank was huge. It had a large ISAF presence whose mission was to train Afghan National Police. FOB Shank was strategically located within easy Chinook range of the Tangi Valley, which was where the Taliban massed for attacks on Kabul. Even before we received any specific intel briefings, we knew why we were here and had a good idea of what we'd be up against.

In much the same way as Pakistan had basically given up trying to govern their Federally Administered Tribal Areas, Tangi Valley (also known as Wardak Valley) had survived as its own entity for millennia, resisting any invasion or imposition of government control. The mountains there provided an all-but-impenetrable stronghold for the Taliban. The Afghan government was simply too weak to control it, so it was left to us to try to put a dent in the Taliban forces there.

While some questioned the value, given the risks, of going up against these well-entrenched Taliban in their mountain stronghold, the risks of not taking them on were greater. Along with the foreign fighters who flocked to them, the Taliban had enough forces in the area to pose a continuous threat to coalition forces. This ran the gamut from ambushing military convoys to rocket and mortar attacks on coalition bases to seeding roads with IEDs and even intimidating Afghan Army forces to get them to turn against American or coalition forces in "green on blue," attacks.

The hell of it was that we couldn't just fight these bastards to a draw. They knew the United States was eventually going to leave—everyone eventually gave up and bailed out of Afghanistan—so all they had to do was make enough attacks on the government to convince Afghans that once the Americans left, the Talibans' shadow government would come out of the mountains and run the country their way. Much like the IMU up north who we were fighting out of MES, the Taliban in Tangi Valley held the civilian population hostage.

It was the height of the fighting season, and we didn't expect to be buttoned down in FOB Shank for long. We weren't disappointed. Late one afternoon, our platoon sergeant told us to gather our kit and weapons in a hurry and report to TOC. We got a quick intel dump that a midlevel Taliban commander was holed up in a village along with his PSD (personal security detail). That alone told us he was at least upper midlevel, and maybe bucking for a top leadership post.

Given the amount of Taliban activity in the area, our leadership decided that this was going to be a two-platoon mission. 1st Platoon and 2nd Platoon got the call. Just after dark, following the briefing in TOC and all the other normal preps, we boarded our 160th SOAR Chinooks. It was less than a 30-minute flight to the target area. 1st Platoon's HLZ was 10 klicks to the east of the objective and 2nd Platoon's was 10 klicks to the west. Our tactic was to establish a cordon on open ground to the north of the village and then move through what our intel told us were grassy fields.

When we got to our release point we realized these grassy fields were actually elephant grass. This was exactly like what you see in Vietnam war movies—grass of chest height or higher that slapped you as you pushed through it.

Chris and I planned to split forces once we reached the village: he would hunt the gaps from the ground along the footpaths on the perimeter of the village, where we had security elements—mostly our mortar team and machine gunners.

I was eager to get into the village and follow along with the assault force. I was carrying a pistol, since I knew I'd be climbing buildings and a pistol was just the right weapon for clearing rooftops, as well as little cupolas and stairwells. I was also carrying a load of grenades, a tomahawk, and, of course, Miss America. Chris was armed with a pistol, some grenades, his SR-25, and a sheath knife.

The village reminded me of the illustrations in a Doctor Seuss book. It was a crazy mash-up of curving adobe structures, twisting footpaths, random goat paths, little streams and irrigation ditches, and some two-track roads that were basically just wider footpaths that were passable by small vehicles. The entire place defied logic, serving only whatever specific purposes these villagers and their predecessors had had when they built it.

When we got to the exterior of the first compound, I found a wooden ladder and used it to clamber up to a rooftop to get a good vantage point of the entire compound and the surrounding area. I was looking for enemy snipers or any signs of an ambush from the village immediately to the south or the fields in the other directions.

From my vantage point I watched 1st Platoon conduct its surreptitious breach, slipping a Ranger inside to open the vehicle gate. I moved to what amounted to a second-story rooftop on top of the compound's living quarters. Soon Zeke was on his bullhorn relaying instructions for Two-Seven, Platoon Sergeant Pack.

I turned my attention to the rest of the village, scanning in a sweeping pattern. The columns of cypress trees and short canopies of fruit trees fouled my view. I cinched up my sling so that Miss America was tight and horizontal against my chest plate of ballistic body armor and switched to my handheld thermal imager. This indispensable little device picks up what infrared night vision cannot, but it didn't do me much good here. The foliage was just too dense.

"Sierra-One, Seven." It was Platoon Sergeant Pack over the net. I knew they were wrapping up their search of this compound and there was a lot of ground to cover tonight, so the platoon needed to move as fast as it could.

"Go for, Sierra," I replied, letting him know I was ready for his transmission.

"We have a sparkle coming down on our next target building," he said. (A sparkle is a drone with IR capability.) "You see anything?"

Overhead, the drone washed the compound to our south in a bright green glow. I scrutinized the area for several seconds. Nothing.

"Negative, Seven," I replied. "I have eyes but no movement, and I can't see much. Too many trees."

"Roger, Sierra. Seven out," Pack replied.

I listened as he began organizing the platoon for a move into the village to the south, issuing quick instructions. In the last few months I'd gained more trust, and with it autonomy, from Platoon Sergeant Pack. He knew that I'd always be somewhere nearby, lurking on a rooftop or stalking among his men, finding the things they couldn't see, confirming information related to us from the various aircraft overhead.

This is important for any sniper, and especially for me. I don't just need to be useful to him. He also has to trust me to know where the platoon's lines are and to stay out of their way. Every night we went out, he had to keep all these positions in his head. If anyone was in the wrong place—especially me—we'd end up with friendly fire, and the blame for that would rest primarily on his shoulders and those of the other platoon leaders. It didn't escape me how much leeway I had. Without that trust I would have had to clear every movement over the radio, clogging up the net and slowing down the operation.

I tried to memorize all the likely routes—at least the ones I could see—before climbing down. I knew that I'd have narrow fields of fire from the ground, but I hoped I would be able to see farther down those shooting lanes.

The net cleared and I called up Seven.

"Seven, Sierra."

"Go for, Seven."

"Not much point in climbing here. I'll be with ISO," I said, referring to the Rangers who were surrounding the compound of interest to make sure we had security outside the walls.

For all the trust we had, he did need to know which of his elements I'd be closest to. Losing a man or leaving someone behind would also fall squarely on his shoulders, and we all used the buddy system to keep that from happening.

"Roger, Seven out," he replied, as he turned his attention back to the complex task of moving armed men through the twisting village in the dark.

Back on the ground, I linked up with ISO. I walked up to Staff Sergeant John, call sign Two-Three, the ISO squad leader.

"Hey, Sierra!" he began, greeting me with a big grin. "Fighting with us tonight?"

"That's right, War Bro!" I replied, catching his enthusiasm. I knew John from his Recce days, and we had a friendship forged in fire.

"Nice," he said, as he pumped his fist and moved out behind his Alpha Team Leader. I let the rest of his squad pass and then fell in behind his Bravo Team.

We surrounded the compound, and John set up his men on the perimeter.

I hung back a bit and waited for the now-routine takedown of this compound to begin. When I heard Zeke's bullhorn, I walked first to one end of Sergeant John's lines and then to the other, to see where I could do the most work.

I decided that I needed to move closer to the center of the village to get the best field of fire for Miss America.

There was a clearing between the trees and a proper orchard about 100 meters on one side. From my position I had a clear view of a well-trod footpath. I narrowed my focus on the footpath: it could provide the enemy with a high speed avenue of approach or a perfect avenue of escape.

The 4-foot berms here made for good fighting positions. There was a SAW gunner near me, and I let him know I was going to push out a little farther and do some hunting. He nodded and confirmed the direction in which I would head. We would fight together as a buddy team if it hit the fan.

I followed a twisting footpath and moved about 50 meters away.

My earpiece cracked loudly: "Squirters heading east."

"South of the target building, heading for 1st Platoon," came the call.

I'd been moving north, and now I turned on a heel and headed back toward our SAW gunner.

"Two-Three, that's your left limit," Platoon Sergeant Pack, call sign Two-Seven, called out, telling me the action was likely coming my way. I was at the left limit of Staff Sergeant John's isolation squad. I marveled at how Seven kept all of this in his head in the heat of battle.

"Two-Three, Sierra," I began. "I have your SAW gunner. We'll intercept."

"Roger, Sierra, moving your way with backup," Sergeant John called back to me. It didn't escape me that I had just taken control of Sergeant John's most casualty-producing weapons and a young Ranger he was responsible for, and he didn't hesitate or question me. That's the kind of trust you only get from always bringing your A game when it counts, and we had been doing that in spades for months now.

"SAW, let's move up to the intersection," I said. There was no need to use his name—he knew what weapon he had in his hand. Maybe it's just the way my brain is wired, but when I'm in the heat of battle I think in terms of weapons rather than people. I didn't need "Gary" to come with me; I needed a Squad Automatic Weapon.

I flashed my laser at a pile of fill-dirt that was almost as tall as a man. It would provide both of us with good cover so we could see down the east-west-running high-speed avenue of approach.

We got to that position and soon saw shadowy figures flashing through the trees and mounds running in an east-northeast direction toward us. It took me a minute to get a solid count: there were three of them.

We couldn't see weapons, and we didn't have a shot. We were alone in the center of a hostile village, so we kept our triggers tight but didn't fire. Two of the men disappeared, but the third man continued on his east-northeast trajectory toward us. When he hit the large east-west-running footpath, I sent a shot into the packed ground near his feet. The round sprayed dirt and rocks up into the air and the man jumped like a character in a Looney Tune cartoon, then used the footpath to make a high-speed escape.

I trusted my suppressor, along with the man's panic, to keep our position concealed, but I knew that my shot would send him into 1st Platoon's lines to the east and that they would be watching that footpath. If I let him continue heading in a northerly direction, he would twist and turn through the maze of buildings and pop up somewhere impossible to predict at the edge of the village, where Chris and a small team were watching. If it sounds like I was herding him, I was. I wanted to send him right to our machine-gun team instead of letting him sneak around in the village and pop up somewhere unexpected.

"Sierra, what are you engaging?" It was my captain's voice crackling across the net.

"Warning shot," I replied. "I'm sending him east on Phase Line Broncos."

"Roger," he replied. My captain had been there and done that as a former enlisted man, so he knew exactly what I was doing and why I was doing it. He switched a dial on his radio and called the 1st Platoon's leader, "Squirters inbound on Phase Line Broncos, heading toward 1st Platoon."

We didn't chase the squirters down. If we had, we could have ended up running straight into 1st Platoon's fire. Also, we knew 1st Platoon could handle them.

Meanwhile, inside the compound, the tactical questioning was going well and we were extracting the intel we needed. The occupants of the compound told us that there was someone who they thought was a Taliban leader living in a compound on the outskirts of another village, just 500 meters to our northwest.

Platoon Sergeant Pack called up Two-Three and tasked his squad with moving to that compound. If the Taliban leader became alerted to our presence, Two-Three and our new terp, who'd been shadowing Zeke for the last few missions, would try to stop them. Two-Three, Staff Sergeant John, was going to take his squad and a terp to the northwest to get a cordon around the Taliban boss's house.

I linked up with Sergeant John's SAW gunner and called Seven to let him know that Chris was going to swap out with me. I reviewed the plan with Chris over the net, and he sent back an eager "Roger." As far as hunting goes, he was a bit hamstrung by the elephant grass and low terrain on the edge of the building. I knew it was a lot more interesting to poke around in the village than to stare into the distance, providing overwatch and listening to a radio in his ear. I gave him a few details about what I'd seen, and he moved into the village with the rest of the outer cordon.

Sergeant John and I chatted quickly about how I planned to cover him. There was a tall hill, almost 100 feet high, and I figured I'd be able to provide covering sniper fire from there. More important, since he couldn't see anything that wasn't right in front of him because of the trees and the elephant grass, I would be able to alert him if an enemy force was heading toward his position, and he would be able to get back to the main element without detection.

Sergeant John moved out at a trot and his squad fell in behind him. I made my way to the large hill. I knew I'd be pretty well exposed, but there wasn't much terrain around me where the enemy could hide, so I traded concealment for being able to spot any trouble coming my way long before the enemy could effectively engage me. At least that's what I hoped for.

I got to the hill before Two-Three was in position and saw his squad's infrared beacons switch on when they reached a wooded, elephant grass-covered delta at the confluence of two deep irrigation trenches.

Sergeant John's squad moved closer and closer to the compound but was still separated from it by running water in the irrigation trenches. This was a tactical move by a crafty Ranger squad leader to keep any looky-loos from stumbling into them. The bit of ground they were on was swampy and mosquito-ridden, with elephant grass as tall as they were, so I could just make out their positions. I switched to my thermal imager and scanned the area. I needed to call Mac.

"Two-Three, you have inbound. I think they're women and children—too many of them to be fighters," I warned him.

"Okay, can you PID?" he asked, hoping that I could identify weapons if there were fighters hiding in what appeared to be a mass exodus to the east.

"Negative, not at this range," I replied. "If you PID, mark them, and I'll take them down." I knew that Sergeant John or one of his men would use their lasers to mark any enemy they saw. Once they did that, I could go to work with Miss America. This was our usual tactic: we'd have to be each other's eyes and ears.

I suddenly got a sinking feeling as well over a hundred Afghans slowly swarmed out of the village, moving silently and sleepily in the moonlight. We'd learned the hard way that while they could just be villagers fleeing the fighting, any number of them could be wearing suicide vests or be Taliban fighters in disguise, or they could just start a riot and tear John and his squad to shreds. It was a sea of humanity that you can't relate to or communicate with, and we were outsiders, which is inherently dangerous.

"I can hear them, Balls," John whispered over the net. He was barely audible and was using my old nickname, breaking radio protocol. "How far until they're on us?" he asked.

"Fifty meters. I have good eyes," I replied, letting Sergeant John know that they were close enough now for me to see if they were armed men or just women and children fleeing.

"Roger, we'll fight our way back while you lay it down if they cross the creek," Sergeant John whispered back.

"If you hear me cracking overhead, that's my PID," I replied.

I was so far away that Sergeant John wouldn't hear if I fired suppressed rounds, but he would hear the crack of my bullets' supersonic wake as they zipped over his head. It was all the warning I had time for. I wouldn't be able to take my hand off my gun to key my radio if there were fighters I needed to take down, it would happen that fast.

Sergeant John answered in the affirmative by breaking squelch.

I quickly scanned each of the fleeing people and started to feel some relief. This *was* a mass exodus; they were all women and children. They were now surrounding John on all sides, and I could see figures from the village who were not women and children. The lights in the Taliban leader's compound had come on as well.

I had a problem. I needed to provide sniper fire for Sergeant John and his squad, but I couldn't do that if armed men got tangled up with the women and children. That, in a nutshell, described the difference between us and them. If women and children get caught in a cross fire, the Taliban's attitude is "so be it," and they'll even use civilian deaths for propaganda purposes. Conversely, we'll do anything we can to prevent that from happening. At that range, without a spotter, the risk of my hitting a woman or a child would be too great for me to accept.

After a short time, the mass of people moved past Sergeant John and his Rangers.

The exodus moved past me to the north and joined another mass of women and children beating feet to the east.

"Two-Three, you're clear, but you have MAMs moving in and out of the compound," I called out, not trying to hide the urgency in my voice.

Before I could get a good count, Sergeant John was up and splashing his way through the chest-deep canal. His inexperienced interpreter hesitated, but the rest of the squad followed him to the Taliban leader's house.

"America! Come out with your hands up!" Sergeant

John shouted. His red laser danced on a man near the doorway of the compound's walls as he smashed his way out of the water.

"America!" he yelled again, and then, in his hillbilly version of Pashtun, he added, "Hands up; let me see your hands!"

John was a crazy bastard that night, and his brazen move confounded even his squad, but they dutifully cleared the canal and spread out to surround the men in the compound.

"Everyone knows what 'America' means," he explained to me later at FOB Shank when I asked him what he'd been thinking.

John's terp finally got his head back in the game and was shouting practiced instructions in Pashtun, telling the men in the compound exactly what to do. His bullhorn was useless after having been dunked during the water crossing.

Meanwhile, Platoon Sergeant Pack was wrapping things up in the first village we cleared, and he sent a fire team from Two-One to help them take down the Taliban compound. While we had things under control for the moment, six Rangers weren't enough to search a compound, provide external security, and detain and question a large number of personnel.

Suddenly, to my southeast, I heard a cacophony of Soviet-era arms clashing with M4 fire. I slid down my mini-mountain in that direction, trying to get eyes on. I could see Mac and Wade on another steep hill just like mine. I knew they were both using M110s, and I knew what kind of range they could get from that weapon. I heard the whispering noises of their suppressed shots snaking rounds into the darkness.

I flipped to 1st Platoon's net and heard them calling their shots. Armed men were fleeing from 1st Platoon's half of the village, but Mac and Wade cut them down mercilessly. A couple of the fleeing fighters managed to get 900 meters out, but Mac snapped off two rounds in quick succession. They looped through the air before cutting the squirters down at the edge of the open ground they were trying to cross.

Meanwhile, four members of 1st Platoon's 3rd Squad were moving across flat ground through elephant grass when they were ambushed by seven Taliban fighters.

Back on the FOB, I went to the firing range every chance I got, and 3rd Squad was usually there too. Their team leaders and the rest of the squad were absolutely "students of the gun," and that extra commitment to training was paying off now. As soon as the Taliban fighters jumped up, 3rd Squad Leader and Alpha Team Leader registered the shape of their Soviet-era weapons, and both Ranger teams began firing at the same instant.

The Rangers' practiced motions meant that they didn't miss, while the Taliban fighters did. The two Ranger privates, only an instant behind their leader's seasoned reflexes, didn't miss either, and they cut down four of the enemy fighters immediately. The other three Taliban were wounded and fled the hail of bullets, trying to make it to the momentary safety of the village. One never made it. The Alpha Team Leader and the two privates gave chase immediately, while the 3rd Squad leader followed a few steps behind, hurriedly radioing reports of what was happening.

The two remaining Taliban fighters split up. One fled deeper into the village, while the other one, who was carrying a PKM machine gun, ducked behind the walls of a rubbled-out building. His machine gun must have been damaged, or had a malfunction, because he never turned and fired it at them.

The Alpha Team Leader rushed headlong into the building. He could see the Taliban fighter frantically trying to get his machine gun into action, slap home the feed tray cover, and swivel its barrel straight at him. Alpha Team Leader wasn't completely certain where his squad leader was and feared he might be on the other side of the wall. The Alpha Team Leader dropped his M4, letting it hang from its sling. Then he ripped his tomahawk from its sheath and rushed straight at the machine-gun-wielding Taliban fighter, hitting him with two rapid blows. He rode the man to the ground, and his next blow struck somewhere around the man's collarbone. He stood on the man's chest and fired his M4 into the Taliban fighter's face, sure now that the ground beneath them would catch the bullets.

The rest of the night was fairly pro forma. We did our battle damage assessment, destroyed Taliban weapons, and walked out of the village to our HLZ exfil site. If we learned anything on this mission it was that our work here wasn't done. The Taliban were here in numbers and were eager to take us on.

9
EYE ON THE PRIZE

If I this book had been written in strictly chronological order, what I'm going to tell you in this chapter would have already been told several chapters ago.

I attended what is now the Special Forces Sniper Course (SFSC) at Fort Bragg Special Warfare Center (SWC or JFKSWC) late in 2010, three months before our Team Merrill deployment. It had previously been called the Special Operations Target Interdiction Course (SOTIC), and the names are used interchangeably. When I attended the course, I did well enough to be the lead student and in the running for honor grad until the last few weeks, mostly thanks to my partner, Stuart.

Stuart and I were the youngest service members in the course, both by age and rank (we were sergeants, or E-5s, while the rest of the class were E-6 and above), and we also had the least time in service overall. Not only that, but many of the other students were sniper instructors at their various units. Despite having the highest marks in the class for six out of the eight weeks of the course, a sergeant first class who was a marksmanship instructor, and who had three times my time in service, finally surpassed my score.

No excuses here; the sergeant first class was a pro who earned his win. I felt that I had an edge with Stuart as my partner, as he had exceptional knowledge and skill in long-range shooting. He had competed in the President's 100— our nation's most prestigious long-range shooting match for civilians—as a teenager and was a formidable competition long-range shooter prior to his military service.

I was a little disappointed in myself, but after a while I saw the errors I had made during the SOTIC/SFSC course as lessons I couldn't learn anywhere but here and in combat. I had the luxury of making them in a controlled environment under the tutelage of the finest sniper instructors in the most rigorous sniper school on the planet.

I know now, just as I knew during my deployment with Team Merrill, that those hard lessons not only saved my bacon on numerous occasions but also saved the lives of the better men I was tasked with overwatching. Coming so close to being an honor grad and seeing the time and resources my instructors had to refine their knowledge made me covet their job.

I knew then that I might one day have what it took to be a sniper instructor. It seemed like the perfect fit. I could pass on my hard-won combat knowledge, and I would be able to hone my skills even further at these one-of-a-kind facilities surrounded by not only the best instructors but the best students as well. Coming in second in the course planted a seed, and I still feel a sense of pride at having held my own against those giants of men, each of them decorated war heroes many times over.

A few weeks after we completed the SOTIC/SFSC course, Stuart and I were back in Fort Bragg to compete at the Annual Sniper Competition at USASOC (United States Army Special Operations Command). Our competitors were a veritable who's who of Special Operations snipers from a wide array of agencies and units, some with names I can't reveal. It was the Super Bowl of sniper competitions, and we would be competing against the very best and dedicated gunslingers, men who live and die by the long gun.

Going into the competition, I realized that, at least on paper, Stuart and I were the underdogs. Just as in the SOTIC/SFSC course, we were the most junior competitors. Most of the other sniper competitors had two to three times as much time in service as we did, as well as time behind a long gun.

Stuart and I showed up with our service guns. We each had our M110s and our Mk-13s. With Stuart leveraging his uncanny shooting and spotting ability, and with the expert tutelage of the SFSC cadre fresh in our minds, we found ourselves firmly in the lead for the first two days of the competition. As the competition evolved we went back and forth, but in the end we slipped out of the lead, finishing, to our disappointment, in second place.

It was a sniper's dream and the best shooting experience of my life. We were running and gunning and stalking through the urban and jungle terrain in Fort Bragg. When the competition was over we had a large formal banquet and everyone was awarded prizes. The prizes were substantial and generous. Stuart and I were on a high at the banquet, and there was a good reason for it.

The day before, we had a chance to talk with the Cadre running the competition, many of whom had been our instructors from the SOTIC/SFSC course. We told them we were disappointed with second place and that it felt like losing. The NCOIC (NonCommissioned Officer In Charge) was quick to "adjust" our negative attitude.

He told us that not only did we "look like shit on paper" compared with our older, more experienced competition but we had defied all expectations as two young "buck sergeants" (the old Army's term for young sergeants). He patiently explained that anyone who "showed" here (meaning a top three finish) was a winner. "By tonight, you will feel like a winner. Wait until we hand you your guns," he said with a big smile.

That grizzled master sergeant had a way of smoothing the edge of our disappointment. He had the experience and the savvy to put our accomplishment in perspective, and he was right. We ran the field, but in the end the more experienced team won. It took the very real weight of our holding our new custom rifles and scopes in our hands as we stood for a picture next to the USASOC Commander, General Mulholland, before what we had done really sank in. Most snipers never get the chance to compete in a military-wide competition. Fewer still get a chance to go toe-to-toe with the real-life version of men that video games and movies are based on.

After the banquet, we celebrated to excess with Marc (later my Team Merrill partner) and our sniper platoon sergeant. They had placed somewhere in the middle of the pack, still a feat to be proud of. Heck, just being chosen to field a team was an honor. Our celebration was colored by the anxious uncertainty we felt knowing we'd be in Afghanistan putting these skills to the test in just a few short months.

Throughout my deployment with Team Merrill, the seed that had been planted in SOTIC/SFSC as a student, and nurtured by the breakout performance Stuart and I had in the USASOC competition, continued to grow. During our base-hopping, the sniper team that had edged us out for first place even sought me out to come along on one of their sniper missions. Mac went too, and I was glad he did. Working alongside those men during combat turned that seed into a sprout.

By the time we were at FOB Shank at the end of our seven-month tour, I knew I had to take one more long shot. I had always wanted to be a sniper instructor, and the herniated disks in my aching back agreed with my heart. I couldn't help thinking, after all the impossible odds we had survived, that maybe, just maybe, I could be a sniper instructor for the Special Forces Sniper Course. It was something that had never been done before: a Ranger had never become an instructor at the Special Forces Sniper Course. But it was worth everything to me—up to insubordination—to try to do it.

I don't know if it's this way throughout the regular Army, but within the 75th Ranger Regiment, mentorship was something that went with the territory. I was the beneficiary of that mentorship from two great NCOs, Platoon Sergeant Pack and First Sergeant Hutch. Each of them would meet with me informally and have in-depth conversations about where my career was going. It takes time to gain trust, especially so you can broach the subject of making your own job. But they both genuinely cared about my career, as well as my health, and wanted to help me reach my full potential in the military.

Throughout Team Merrill's deployment, slowly, mission after mission, I gained their trust and confidence. By the end of the deployment, that impression was positive enough that they were willing to lobby the Command Sergeant Major of the 75th Ranger Regiment to recommend me for a position as an instructor at the Special Forces Sniper School. Toward the end of July, their mentorship sessions with me became more pointed. They grilled me to ensure that I'd be able to explain to anyone why I was uniquely qualified for this assignment. They also formulated a plan of attack to give me the best shot at fulfilling my professional dream.

I admit that even with Platoon Sergeant Pack and First Sergeant Hutch in my corner, I was intimidated by the prospect of being interviewed by CSM Merritt, the 75th Ranger Regiment's Command Sergeant Major. He was a legend, with vast combat experience and military schooling that could fill volumes.

CSM Merritt was also a ruthless warrior and single-minded in his commitment to one thing: Rangers. He was pushing forty, but he would come to your pre-Ranger selection or Expert Infantry Badge trial and outrun or out-ruck march you and the rest of the teenagers and twenty-somethings who were trying out. And he did it barefoot! He told us he ran and rucked barefoot because if he was ever captured by the enemy, when they took his boots it wouldn't stop him from escaping. Most humans can't do Ranger runs at all, and he did them barefoot.

CSM Merritt was scheduled to meet with Team Merrill in FOB Shank at the end of July, and First Sergeant Hutch's game plan was to request an audience with this legendary warrior after our task force sensing session—basically, a survey where we give feedback to the most senior NCO in our regiment. I was so nervous, I wondered if I could just walk back into Musa Qala or the Tangi Valley instead; but I knew this was the only way to reach my goal. With Platoon Sergeant Pack and First Sergeant Hutch backing me up, I did my research, built my case, and practiced making my points.

The night finally came, and I waited patiently while we briefed CSM Merritt on our deployment. I was sure he'd understand the monumental task we had just accomplished. When we had begun this rotation almost seven months ago, we never expected that all of us would be sitting in the same room, physically unscathed, without a single casualty in our ranks. To this day, I still can't believe it.

When the briefing was over and everyone had cleared out, it was time to make my case to CSM Merritt as to why I should be the first Ranger to instruct at the Special Forces Sniper Course. To put this in perspective, we were asking the highest-ranking noncommissioned officer in the 75th Ranger Regiment to call in a favor so that I could get my dream job. I hoped that fortune did, in fact, favor the bold, because this was as audacious as inviting the Taliban to a gunfight in their own backyard.

It took me about two hours to make my case, and CSM Merritt challenged me at every turn. He was the type of senior leader who never forgot what it was like to be a Ranger private, or a sergeant in my position for that matter. He genuinely wanted what was best for each of us in the Regiment, but he balanced that with his solemn duty to do what was best for the Regiment as a whole.

CSM Merritt didn't just take me at my word when I said something, and it was the most grueling discussion I have even been in, going toe-to-toe with this legendary Ranger. He came straight at me, picking apart each of my points, demanding that I justify myself completely. With First Sergeant Hutch advocating beside me, CSM Merritt was finally convinced that this was the best thing for me and, more important, the best thing for the 75th Ranger Regiment.

He explained that there were two ways this could go. I could leave the 75th Ranger Regiment and be assigned to the Special Warfare Center. This meant I would again have to go through the grueling Ranger Selection that had nearly killed me the first time I went through it, when I was five years younger and didn't have spinal injuries. The alternative was that I could remain assigned to the 75th Ranger Regiment and be attached to the school as a liaison instructor.

Not only did he give me his word that he would personally do everything in his power to make sure I would get the assignment—which involved calling in a favor and convincing the Army Special Forces that an outsider should join their prestigious ranks—but he even gave me the choice to do so on my own terms.

When we shook hands I knew I had earned something singular. After he left the briefing room, I sat with First Sergeant Hutch for a few minutes, still in disbelief that we had pulled this off.

"Well, you got what you wanted, Martinez," First Sergeant Hutch said.

"First Sergeant, I . . . I never thought this could happen," I said a bit blankly. "Thank you for helping me with all of it."

I was in complete shock. This was a once-in-a-lifetime opportunity that had arrived completely out of thin air.

Platoon Sergeant Pack and First Sergeant Hutch had stuck their necks out to vouch for me, which they didn't have to do at all.

"You earned this," First Sergeant Hutch said. "With all you did for our platoon this deployment, you deserve it. Pass on your knowledge—you have plenty of it."

It still hadn't sunk in. I had joined the Army just hoping to fight for my country, maybe get my jump wings, and go to a cool-guy school like Ranger School or Sniper School. But First Sergeant Hutch was right. I had been given the knowledge by the best snipers in the Army—Rangers, Sniper School instructors, and Green Berets—and I had taken that knowledge overseas and back. Now I was going to get a chance to pass that on to the men who would be fighting for the foreseeable future and teach at the best sniper school on the planet.

I was overwhelmed, but as I thought back to how I had laid out my case to CSM Merritt, a man I revered and respected absolutely, I began to believe that I was actually prepared for this new challenge.

With the privilege of knowing I'd be going to my dream job once I got back stateside, my last few weeks in Afghanistan with Team Merrill were full of anticipation. We spent my last day or two palletizing our gear. This meant we inventoried and packed all our things, minus my M4, body armor, and a single large assault pack. I also packed an overnight bag with comfort items for the trip home: a poncho liner, or "woobie"; an iPod; a couple of books; hygiene stuff; documents for customs; copies of the inventory I had packed in our pallets; a clean uniform; and a set of PT gear.

I knew that unless the base got overrun, I was free and clear. As soon as it was dark we'd be going to the airfield to get on a C-17 military transport and head home. We'd make a quick stop at Ganci Air Base in Manas, Kyrgyzstan, then fly straight to Fort Benning.

I headed to our TOC to make sure we were up-to-date on our timelines and to send emails to coordinate with our chain of command in the States. Going home meant that I'd be back under Headquarter Company's command and I needed to reestablish myself in their routine. They were my parent company and had loaned me out to Team Merrill.

When I got to the TOC my heart raced. I quickly learned we had TIC in the Tangi Valley. We looked at the blurry drone feed of the fighting at the mouth of the valley. We hoped that they were delivering the knockout punch that Team Merrill had spent the last few weeks setting up in the flat plains surrounding that hotly contested valley. We didn't have time to fixate on the live feed—we had the rest of our retrograde/redeployment tasks to complete, and we were on an unforgiving timeline.

Still, it was a tense and solemn moment for all of us. We knew the danger our Ranger brothers were in, and our natural instinct was to help. We learned that another Ranger platoon, from 1st Battalion, was on standby to be their QRF.

I pulled myself away from the immediate crisis and tried to focus on the last few tasks at hand. I did my final packing, and Chris and I double-checked each other's work, strictly adhering to the Ranger buddy system of checking and double-checking everything. Even though our flight back to the States was in less than 24 hours, we needed to maintain the kind of discipline that had gotten us through this rotation.

Every so often, one of the Rangers from 2nd Platoon came by and gave us updates on the firefight, as well as on our own timeline to head to the airfield. We learned that our TIC were meeting heavy resistance, and our leadership had decided to launch the QRF. We also learned that a team of SEALs were going to go in as well. Their mission was to run down a Taliban leader, his personal security detail, and a group of fighters traveling with them.

Once all my retrograde/redeployment tasks were complete, I made my way over to the SEALs TOC. I had done some hunting on the previous deployment with a SEAL sniper I only knew as Rat, and I heard it was his team that was going to bolster our Ranger QRF. I just happened to catch him coming out of the SEAL TOC in full kit, sniper rifle in hand. He still had the cut-down breach-action shot-gun that looked just like a pirate's blunderbuss that I remembered from our last hunting trip together. Seeing this seasoned killer in his well-worn battle gear put a smile on my face.

"Rat!" I called out. It took him a minute to recognize me in my clean garrison uniform.

"Hey, Balls, your boys found some trouble! You're not coming?" he said with a wry grin.

I just chuckled. "Not this time. I'm heading back to Benning tonight."

He shrugged lightly. I put out my hand and we grabbed each other's forearms in a Spartan handshake.

"Good shit, man. Maybe we'll see you on the next rotation," Rat replied.

"Hope so, Rat. Happy hunting, brother," I said. We released each other's forearms and turned away to go about our business.

I made my way back to our side of the FOB, and we eventually headed out to the airfield. We were completely in the dark about what was happening in the Tangi Valley. It was frustrating, to say the least: we were warriors and fighters, our brothers were in hot combat, and not only couldn't we help but we had as little idea about what was happening as someone sitting in the comfort of their home in the States.

We boarded the C-17, packed in tight, and bundled against the cold, high-altitude flight. Our doc passed out some sleep aids, and as I slipped into the deep, medicated blackness, I had no thoughts.

It wasn't until we got back to Fort Benning that we found out about the tragedy that had been visited on our fellow warriors. A National Guard Chinook—call sign Extortion Seventeen—had been hammered out of the sky by an RPG on its final approach to an uncleared LZ. All thirty-eight men on board, as well as one military working dog, were killed instantly.

A second National Guard Chinook with the Ranger

QRF had to scramble to find another LZ about 20 kilometers away. The Ranger Platoon that was on the ground, and that had been in bitter fighting with the Taliban, managed to finally break through the resistance that had trapped them and moved out with one mission in mind: to recover the bodies at the crash site.

They cut a bloody swath through fanatical Taliban fighters who seemed to swarm from every compound they passed. The Taliban had the same goal: to get to the American bodies and desecrate them. In one of the most heroic marches in the annals of U.S. military operations, Rangers pushed through what was then the most dangerous place in Afghanistan, fighting the Taliban along the way and making a headlong dash to the crash site.

The Ranger platoon made it to the crash site first, leaving a wake of dead Taliban, and recovered our SEAL brothers and the Extortion Seventeen crew. The Ranger QRF that was forced to land 20 kilometers from the crash site, now secured, finally made it there and went immediately about their bitter work. They recovered every SEAL, crewman, JTAC, and Afghan Commando, as well as the K-9.

There was no way to feel good about this mission, but it was some solace to know we didn't leave any of our fallen comrades behind.

There's no better way I can capture what it means to be a Special Operator. Team Merrill spent seven months in Afghanistan engaged in some of the heaviest fighting imaginable, and remarkably, *miraculously*, we didn't lose a Ranger. We could deconstruct every mission and point to a half-dozen things that could have gone differently each time that would have caused us to lose men.

On the other hand, the loss of Extortion Seventeen and all thirty-eight men on board to an enemy RPG—just one Taliban who was in the right place at the right time—put an exclamation mark on how we live on the edge of disaster, with only dumb luck on our side and our Ranger buddies looking out for us.

ACKNOWLEDGMENTS

My special thanks go to my Ranger brother Nicholas Irving, who is the only reason I ever had the opportunity to write this book, and for killing that one guy who was going to kill me back in "Taliban City." Thanks, Reaper!

To my editor, Marc Resnick, who went to incredible lengths to make this book happen. He was truly the man behind the scenes.

To my coauthor, George Galdorisi, for working with me on this story. Like most Ranger missions, this one couldn't have been done without a helo pilot.

To my exceptional designer and close friend Lisa Pompileo, you truly gave 100 percent and then some.